*Constitutionalism
and Resistance
in the Sixteenth Century*

Constitutionalism
and Resistance
in the Sixteenth Century

Three Treatises by Hotman, Beza, & Mornay

Translated and edited by
Julian H. Franklin

PEGASUS NEW YORK

To the memory of Franz L. Neumann

Contents

Introduction

The medieval background

The works represented in this volume are landmarks in the history of political thought because they constitute a clear and definite transition from medieval to modern constitutionalist ideas. The constitutionalism associated with the Germanic kingships of the early Middle Ages was generally limited to the right of active resistance—by the whole community or any part—against a ruler who in his judgments or his edicts had come into serious conflict with the sense of justice embodied in the folk tradition. The supremacy of law, in other words, was not guaranteed by regular institutional controls. As long as he could maintain the effective consent of the community, a king could act upon his own discretion, for even if he were expected to consult with the magnates or wise men of the realm before making any great decision, he was not bound to do so and was also free, at least in principle, to choose his advisers as he pleased.[1] Moreover, the acknowledged right to resist, or even overthrow, a king does not seem to have been regarded as an act of the community, done in its corporate capacity, against a ruler whose authority, as a mandatory of the people, could be revoked by it for cause. An "unjust king" was simply set aside *de facto* and a successor confirmed by some form of acclamation and rendering of homage.[2] Hence the notion of the supremacy of law, although deeply rooted in the early medieval tradition, was not associated with two ancillary concepts that are fundamental to modern constitutionalism—the idea of a sovereign community from which all authority derives, and the institutionalization of that sovereignty through control of governmental power by the people or their representatives.

With the transition to the more complex and organized institutions of the high and later Middle Ages, both of these ideas appeared.[3] From the eleventh century on, the principle of popular sovereignty became increasingly familiar as a result of the revival of Roman law and the scholastic study of classical philosophy. All of the commentators on Roman civil law interpreted the *lex regia** of the *Digest* of Justinian to mean that the emperor's authority ultimately derived from a grant of the community. Many, although by no means all, held this grant to be revocable for cause on the ground of a private-law analogy to the people as the principal and the emperor as its agent.[4] And there were even some who believed that the people had retained, in principle at least, some share of legislative power.[5] Similar conclusions, further, could be, and sometimes were, arrived at by theologians and philosophers who took Aristotle rather than the Roman Law as the starting point for political discussion. Perhaps the most radical statement of popular sovereignty in the Middle Ages is the *Defensor pacis* of Marsilius of Padua, which, building on Aristotle, attributed the ultimate legislative power to the people or its *pars valentior.*

The idea of institutional restraints on royal power, on the other hand, was associated with the rise and development, in the high Middle Ages, of representative Estates assemblies. In these bodies, which were to be found under diverse names in almost every part of Western Europe, the base of the older, feudal forms of consultation was expanded to include deputations from the more important towns and sometimes other segments of society that had become politically significant, so

---

*The term used in the *Corpus juris* for the *lex de imperio* by which the people and the Senate were supposed to have given all power to the emperor at the beginning of each reign. The best known formulation is *Digest, I, 4, 1* (from Ulpian): "The pleasure of the prince has the force of law because, by passing the royal law concerning his authority, the people transfers to him and vests in him all of its authority and power." See also *Codex, I, 17, 1, 7.*

that the Estates assemblies began to appear as representations
of the community at large. The consent of the Estates was
normally requisite for new taxation. And in view of the constantly increasing financial needs of more centralized adminis-
trations, these representative bodies could, under favorable
circumstances, demand and even temporarily secure recognition of a number of prerogatives designed to guarantee their
influence—including not only consent to legislation, but also
periodic meetings and rights of judicial and administrative
supervision. Hence in areas especially favorable to this development, we begin to find discussions of the constitutional role of
the Estates in learned literature of the later Middle Ages. In
the kingdoms of Spain, where the political prerogatives of the
Estates were especially extensive, there are commentaries on
the Cortes of Castile and Aragon by cultivated jurists trained
in Roman and Canon Law. In England the Estates were almost
equally as powerful and were to prove more deeply rooted.
In Sir John Fortescue's *Governance of England,* the parliamentary monarchy is given formal classification as a *dominium
politicum et regale,* as opposed to a simple *dominium regale,*
and it is recommended as the form of government that best
maintains the supremacy of law and promotes the common
good.

Yet neither conception in the later Middle Ages was fully
equivalent to the principle of modern constitutionalism. The
idea of the continuing supremacy of the people is, to begin
with, a somewhat exceptional position among the civilians and
the Aristotelians, the more standard view being that of St.
Thomas, for whom ultimate authority is somehow shared by
the king and the community. Even among the more radical
theorists, the central focus is on the jurisdictional conflict
between state and Church, rather than on the constitutional
organization of the Empire or of the territorial kingdoms. Thus
the main point of Marsilius' *Defensor pacis* is to show that the
ruler, as agent of the laity, may intervene to discipline the
clergy. But beyond the brief assertion that rulers ought to be
elected and that rulers may be deposed for tyranny, there is

little examination in Marsilius of their constitutional responsibilities or of any specific devices for enforcing them.

It would appear, therefore, that the only developed assertion of constitutional responsibility within the mainstream of medieval legal and scholastic thought is the conciliarist argument that the whole power of governing the Church is vested in the congregation of the faithful as represented by a General Council. The secular parallel is natural, and it is sometimes noted, in the course of argument, that the people, or the Estates, are above the king and may depose a king for tyranny. But analogies like this are brief and allusive annotations of a case that depends almost exclusively on canonical authorities.* Furthermore, there is no suggestion that these occasional parallels between state and Church were thought to be particularly exact. Hence the immediate effect of conciliarist doctrine on the secular domain turns out to be relatively slight.

The truth, indeed, is that the medieval Estates, whose prerogatives on occasion were extensive, had not been transformed into effective alternatives to royal government and were not so regarded by the leading commentators. The consent of Parliament, according to Fortescue, is required primarily for new taxation and, though less emphatically, for major statutory changes. But there is no suggestion of a general power to control the government. Similarly, for Pedro Belluga, an official of the Cortes of Valencia and a leading commentator on the law of Aragon, the consent of the Cortes is required for change in the *fueros,* or common privileges of the realm. Since these had been conceded by the king in consideration of monetary subsidies, they are regarded as *leges pactionatae,* or laws created by a contract, which cannot be altered unilaterally, at least in ordinary circumstances.[6] But the king, in principle, can legislate in other areas, and since it is he, not the Cortes, who is the ultimate source of authority, he may, in cases of necessity, even modify the *fueros* and impose extraordinary taxes of his own. Hence, for either commentator the Estates are in principle

---

*Most conciliarist writers do not require a theory of the secular constitution since, unlike Marsilius, who is also a conciliarist, they do not admit the power of secular authorities to control the Church.

consultative assemblies whose consent is nonetheless required for certain kinds of royal actions. Whether these actions were numerous or few, the king was limited rather than controlled[7]; and "sovereignty," accordingly, was shared.

Thus, although medieval political ideas often anticipate modern constitutionalism, they are not yet systematically combined into a clear conception of effective control by the community. But in the political crises touched off by the spread of the Reformation in Northern Europe a new combination was precipitated. It emerges most clearly and fully in France, not only because religious conflicts there were especially bitter and protracted, but also because the programs of religious parties were often very closely linked to proposals for political reform.

The political aspect of the French religious wars

On the eve of the French religious wars, which flared intermittently from 1562 to 1598, the institutions of the French establishment, lay as well as clerical, were inefficient and corrupt. The royal treasury was in a chronic state of debt as a result of an expensive military policy, a lavish style at court, and generous patronage to noble favorites. During the reign of Francis I in the early part of the century, the Gallican Church, already infected with sinecures and simony, was transformed into a reservoir of patronage shared among the crown, the great nobles, and the Pope. By the middle of the sixteenth century, the energies of the Church had been so far sapped by absenteeism, that in many parts of France it had simply ceased to function and had lost its contact with the masses. The great administrative bodies, of which the Parlement of Paris was the chief, had been subjected to similar abuses. Judicial and financial offices had long tended to become the vested interests of private persons, but by the sixteenth century, they were systematically and openly venalized to meet financial needs and, for this purpose, cynically multiplied. And while complaints about the complexity and abuses of administrative procedure were traditional, with the venalization of offices indignation was drastically increased.[8] The judicial administration was now regarded by the public less as an institution for dispensing justice than as a device for milking litigants and selling special favors, and the fiscal administration was thought of as a semi-institutionalized system of extortion and embezzlement.

These abuses, furthermore, were bitterly resented, not only by the unprivileged strata of society but by the mass of the nobility as well.[9] The petty squires of the countryside had suffered from an economic squeeze. The monetary yield of their estates was in relative decline, while the expenses of their station were increasing. Most of them accordingly looked to military service as a means of sustenance. But this employment had been seriously reduced by the peace of 1558 with Spain. Their distress was all the more acute because funds were lacking to pay even the wages and pensions due them from the past.

Finally, those classes who stood, in varying degrees, outside the circle of privilege and patronage were relatively less able than before to bear the costs of government. A trade depression, complicated in its causes and felt acutely by contemporaries, diminished both the capacity and willingness of artisans and merchants to pay existing tailles, let alone consent to new ones. The peasants, on whom the main burden of the taille had always fallen, were in even worse condition. Not only had the taille quadrupled since the beginning of the century,[10] but now, as in the past, the method of collection was extremely arbitrary. The result, in the middle of the century, was a palpable decline in agricultural production marked by flight of the peasants from the land in those areas where the burden of taxation seemed intolerable. The agricultural crisis, furthermore, had adverse effects on the interests of other classes, and many members of those classes were aware of them. Merchants blamed the taille and its effects on agriculture for much of the decline in trade. Noblemen complained of the inability of peasants to remit their feudal rents. And the towns were faced with an influx of mendicants and refugees who posed a serious threat to civil order.

At the general Estates of 1560 and 1561, the deputies of the nobility and of the Third Estate were all but unanimous in blaming their troubles on the crown and urgently insisted on reform.* They demanded that older methods of appointment in the Church be restored and that ecclesiastical discipline be enforced so that the way for reconciliation with the Protestants might be prepared. The Church was also expected to increase its contributions to the treasury. Judicial and administrative abuses were to be remedied by the suppression of venality and the improvement of procedures. But general administrative reform was demanded most of all as the ultimate key to fiscal solvency. According to the opinion of the times, the king should and could live off his own, since the royal domain, if properly managed, would yield sufficient income for a prudent household and administration. The depletion of the treasury, accordingly, was attributed to wasteful and corrupt administration. State expenses had been unreasonably increased by the creation of unnecessary offices and the payment of excessive pensions. Much of the domain revenue had been handed out to favorites. And even so, receipts were lower than they ought to be since so much was siphoned off by corrupt and poorly supervised officials. But sincere reform could hardly be expected from the crown, which was surrounded by favorites and flatterers. Frenchmen of the period came increasingly to think that the Estates alone could enforce the necessary changes and that they should therefore meet with regularity.**

This solution to the crisis, although widely accepted at the

---

*The preface to the *Cahier* of the Third Estate in 1560 is bitter and even menacing. "The scandals [of corruption and negligence] that have been imported into this kingdom not so long ago have led everyone with any foresight to believe that it is needful and necessary that your majesty support this fight, this reformation, being assured that the well-being of the kingdom will follow from the resolution to be adopted in this assembly." Charles J. Mayer, *Des Etats Généraux et autres assemblées nationales,* The Hague, 1789, Vol. XI, p. 273. There then follows a list of complaints that is unprecedented in length and detail, running 200 pages and including 354 articles. The *Cahiers* of the other Estates are also impressive in this respect.

**Thus at the Estates of Pontoise in 1561, the *noblesse* demanded, among other things, the right to approve members of the king's council and assemblage of the Estates General every second year. Paul van Dyke, "The Estates of Pontoise," *English Historical Review,* Vol. XXVIII, 1913, pp. 493–494.

time, was surely over-optimistic. High cost and inefficiency were endemic to royal government since the monarchy depended on a privileged nobility whose status was increasingly maintained, directly or indirectly, by military employment, gifts and pensions, and grants of royal domain. Even the privileges of the bourgeois magisterial elite and the specially favored towns could not be seriously altered without endangering the entire system of privilege to which the government was bound. Hence, administrative abuses, ecclesiastical corruption, and excessive burdens on the poor were linked so closely to the social structure that only limited reform was possible. Even then the general Estates—loose in organization, cumbersome in procedure, and generally less developed than their English counterpart—could be only sporadically effective in forcing the government to act.

Political disaffection, therefore, might not have produced any serious opposition to the crown had it not been sustained and organized by factional alignment of the aristocracy and the formation of religious parties. With the death of Henry II in 1559, the crown of France passed in succession to three weak and even mentally unstable kings, of whom the first two were children when they reached the throne, and the last, after 1584 the sole male survivor of the Valois line, was incapable of having children. Throughout this period, accordingly, control of the government and ultimately the crown itself were objects of contention among the leading princely houses, which thus became natural foci of political and religious discontent.

By the middle of the century, moreover, Calvinist dissent had reached a sizeable minority of Frenchmen, including such influential strata as the humanist elite and the urban bourgeoisie, for whom it was especially attractive. With the accession of converts from the nobility in considerable numbers, a political phenomenon emerged which was without precedent in European politics. There now existed an opposition party, drawn from every important stratum of society and from almost every part of France, which was held together by a common principle and was ultimately to be organized by provincial and regional leagues. After 1576, but especially after 1584, a

Catholic counterpart appeared with the formation of the Holy League, which demanded, in opposition to the government, the enforcement of religious uniformity and attempted to insure the succession of a Catholic king.[11] Both religious parties, finally, were inclined at certain times to embrace programs of political and institutional reform, if only as a natural result of their strategic situations. The Huguenots, as a minority, could not hope to attain their basic goal without appeal to discontented Catholics and thus to the nation as a whole. Since a large minority, and perhaps a majority, of Catholics preferred religious compromise to civil war, the League too resorted to political appeals in order to gain support for its religious program.

The Francogallia

These, then, are the circumstances that help to explain the dramatic impact of François Hotman's *Francogallia* when it appeared in 1573. The political message of the work, however, is not conveyed in the form of a polemic composed for a particular occasion, or even of a treatise on the state. The *Francogallia*, rather, is a humanist investigation of French constitutional antiquities by a great scholar who was one of the leading jurists of his age. In an unpublished treatise of 1567 on the reform of legal education, Hotman had called for a study of the native law of France, and especially its public law, in part to show that it embodied universal wisdom and in part also to understand its special characteristics.[12] In the *Francogallia*, the highly sophisticated documentary technique initially developed by the humanists to restore and interpret the sources of classical antiquity is applied to a reconstruction and illustration of the ancient public law of France.

But this legal antiquarianism was also highly programmatic. In the historical perspective of the humanists, the ancient texts and documents were not the remnants of a primitive age, but the venerable monuments of culture which had often been buried or obscured in the course of time. Hotman was returning to the sources in order to restore their pristine meaning and to recover their wisdom for the present. His showing, therefore, that the arrangement established by "our forefathers" was a mixed constitution in which authority was shared between the king and the community was intended and was understood as a political pronouncement on the present. This goal, indeed, is more or less expressly stated at the very beginning of the work and is unmistakable, if not explicit, in almost every passage of the chapters on constitutional arrangements. The characteristics of the ancient constitution are thus presented as a standard against which subsequent changes must be measured and evaluated. Alterations that are in flagrant contradiction are attacked as invalid usurpations.

The first principle, then, of France's constitutional inheritance is that the king is nothing more than a magistrate for life and is constantly subject to removal by the people for violation of the duties of his office. Hotman's proof for this is that the French monarchy was originally elective. Not only was election the tradition of the Franks before they came to Gaul, and of the Gauls before the Roman conquest, but it was also the fundamental act by which the Francogallic commonwealth was constituted. The Frankish monarchy in Gaul was not, in other words, the outcome of a conquest, which might carry implications of arbitrary power. It was the outcome of a free and voluntary association of the Franks and Gauls.* And the act which founded this association was the joint election of a single ruler. From the very beginning, therefore, the kings of France were the creatures and agents of their people. The right of the people to depose not only individual rulers but entire dynasties for incompetence or tyranny is abundantly documented from the early sources.

The law of succession was subsequently altered from election to a complicated order of male primogeniture. This is a modification that Hotman is able to accept. His dominant emphasis in describing the ancient practice of election was not the pro-

---

*Thus although Hotman, as his title indicates, is concerned to show the Germanic-Frankish contribution to French liberties, he does not do so at the expense of the Gallic contribution, and in no way suggests that the Franks were superior to the Gauls either by native inheritance or by right of conquest.

cedural advantages of free selection from a field of candidates.* It was rather the inherent principle that kings are created by the people and are responsible to the people for the conduct of their office. And Hotman carefully preserves this principle in his interpretation of the modified rule. In a brilliant philological critique he shows that the exclusion from the throne of descendants in the female line does not depend upon the Salic law, as was commonly believed, since the Salic law dealt with the inheritance of private property and not with public office.[13] Fixed succession to the throne, accordingly, is not derived from the right to private property, which is completely subject to its owner's will. It is the result of a custom, long observed and accepted by the people, which regulates the order of succession to a public office. The content of the rule, says Hotman very tentatively, may perhaps be understood in terms of feudal law.[14] But it may be noted that even if the kingship were regarded as a fief, it would still be a public office, held of the people as the ultimate owner and subject to definite conditions.

In light of this, there is nothing surprising in Hotman's later use of the law of fixed succession to defend the claim of Henry of Navarre** as heir-apparent. Nor is there any substance to the charge, occasionally heard, that the undertaking was cynical or venal.[15] In his pamphlet of 1585, Hotman argues that, according to the French rule of succession, the son of a deceased older brother (the son would be Henry of Navarre) is preferred over an uncle (Charles de Bourbon, the Catholic candidate) who is the younger brother of the nephew's father.[16]

---

*Even the earliest elections were quasi-dynastic in that preferment was given to the children of the deceased ruler. Despite the quotation from Plutarch (pp. 57–8), Hotman generally approves of this practice.

**Henry of Navarre (1553–1610), the son of Antoine de Bourbon and Jeanne d'Albret, had become king of Navarre on the death of his father in 1572. Although educated as a Protestant, he abjured under constraint after the St. Bartholomew's Day Massacre but then renounced Catholicism after his escape from the French court in 1576. At the death of François, Duke of Anjou, he became heir-presumptive to the throne and was so recognized by Henry III, the last of the Valois, in 1589. Henry of Navarre assumed the title of Henry IV after the death of Henry III in the same year. In 1593 he finally converted to Catholicism and in 1595 was absolved of heresy by Pope Clement VIII.

Hotman here abandons feudal explanations for a more favorable theory based on the intrinsic rights of an apparent heir which he derives from an older commentator, Jean Terre Rouge. But the outcome is in no way devious since the weight of tradition was on Henry's side. And Hotman had always been extremely cautious with his use of feudal explanations.[17] In any case, the point for present purposes is that for Hotman, as for Jean Terre Rouge, succession to the throne still derives from custom, not heredity.[18] The kingship thus remains a public office which the people have given by consent and which they may presumably take away for cause.

In 1585, however, Hotman also published a refutation of the bull of Pope Sixtus V excommunicating Henry, along with the Prince of Condé, and depriving him not only of the kingdom of Navarre but of any right of succession to the throne of France.[19] This too might be considered inconsistent, since the Estates, to whom Hotman gives ultimate power in such matters, had declared in 1577 that no one but a Catholic could be king of France. But here Hotman's position in the *Brutum Fulmen* is that Pope Sixtus, not Henry, is the heretic and that, measured by religious truth, it is the latter not the former who is Catholic; and he makes this appeal to the Estates as though they, together with the Parlements, possess the authority to judge. This is not to say, of course, that Hotman would have given up on Henry's claims if the Estates had specifically debarred him. But even then he would probably have argued against any such decision that it was not a free and legitimate act of the Estates, but the result of coercion by the League.*

Throughout his career, accordingly, Hotman never abandons his position that succession to the crown of France was based on popular consent which could be withdrawn for misbehavior.

---

*Thus Hotman is a letter written in 1589 on an anticipated meeting of the Estates: " The Parisians, for their part, have sent an ambassador to the Pope to ask him to approve their calling the Estates in order to create a new king. . . . All the factious elements, and among them Paris, Toulouse, Lyon, Marseille, Rouen, have convened the Estates for July 15 at Paris." Translated from Rodolphe Däreste, "François Hotman, sa vie et sa correspondance." *Revue Historique*, II, 1876, pp. (1–59, 367–435) p. 428.

The second and more fundamental component of the ancient constitution as Hotman understands it is the public council of the realm, which he hastily assumes remained unaltered in its form from the foundation of the kingdom to his day. In Chapter X, the ancient public council is equated with the Three Estates. The three components of this assemblage are identified with the king, the aristocracy, and the people in a broad analogy to the mixed constitutions of classical antiquity. The clergy, therefore, is not included as a separately organized estate.

Beyond this very rough description we have no further comment on the composition of the public council. But a more precise idea of what Hotman had in mind may be reconstructed from his illustrations. In referring to the constitution of the German Empire, he explicitly identifies the Emperor as the monarchical component, the princes as the aristocratic, and the deputies of the cities and regions *(civitates)* as the popular or democratic element. Similarly, in a description of the public council as it met in France, the only elements distinguished are the king, the princes and the high officials, and the deputations from the towns or regions.[20] We therefore have reason to believe that the aristocratic element, in Hotman's scheme, does not embrace the *noblesse* in its entirety, but only those who hold or have a claim to high position and authority. There is further evidence for this conclusion in a comment on Seyssel,[21] added in the second edition, in which Hotman explicitly rejects the identification of the estates with social orders.*

The popular element, conversely, would refer to all the regional deputies who could in fact be regarded as the elected agents of their particular localities. For even where certain of these deputies were intended to represent the nobility or the clergy,

---

*In modern usage, "estate" refers to a social order, and the three estates are the clergy, the nobility, and the commoners. In the sixteenth century, the terminology is more fluid. The term "estate" is sometimes used for a social order; sometimes for a component of the political order. In the latter case, the first estate would be the King; the second, his high councillors; and the third, the "people," in which not only commoners but lesser nobility and clergy are included without rigid distinction. Hotman normally thinks of the Estates in this latter sense. In addition, it may be noted that Hotman sometimes identifies the Estates with the people and the high councillors only, as when he speaks of the right of the Estates to depose the King.

they were often chosen by the joint vote of all of the Estates assembled in the local *bailliage,* and they often deliberated and voted together at the meeting of the general Estates.[22] Indeed, joint election and joint deliberation became the officially approved procedure with the general Estates of Tours in 1484, which Hotman, like many others at the time, seems to be taking as a model.* For although separation of the three orders for deliberative purposes reappeared at the Estates General of Orleans in 1560, this was regarded as more or less exceptional and did not involve a deliberate rejection of the territorial principle for that of class. Indeed, the procedure in 1560 was apparently the result of a simple refusal of the *noblesse* and commons to sit together with the clergy.** It is also to be noted, finally, that joint election was a common provision in the constitutions of the Huguenot Leagues that were formed around the time the *Francogallia* was written. In what appears to be a frequent arrangement, the delegations from the local units of the League were composed of a stipulated number of gentlemen and commoners who were elected in a common assembly.†

We may conclude, therefore, that it was local or regional delegations of this sort which Hotman had in mind when he

*P. 85, below. Hotman here speaks of an "old," but not original custom of dividing the people into three orders. It is thus regarded as an interlude between the ancient system and the modern and is to be explained by the increasing wealth of the clergy. The explanation may be a reading back into the Estates before Tours a separation from the clergy which occurred in 1560.

**Article 138 in the *Cahier* of the clergy recalls that according to traditional procedure the three orders communicated with each other and presented a single list of grievances through a spokesman of the clergy. But at present, it complains ". . . each of the other two estates have preferred to present their grievances separately through spokesmen from their own estates without any communication with the spokesman chosen by the clergy." Mayer, *op. cit.,* XI, p. 57.

†Thus in the league formed in December, 1573, there was to be an Estates General, which met every six months. And ". . . no persons will be accepted in the said Estates General who have not been deputized by the assembly of the *generalité* [a local administrative unit], to which the principle noblemen of the said *generalité* will [also] be called to elect one [deputy] from the *noblesse* and another from the Third Estate." Eugene and Emile Haag, *La France Protestante,* Paris, 1858, Vol. X, p. 123.

spoke of the popular part of the Estates* and that he looked, not implausibly, on the Estates of his own time as variations on the scheme of Tours. But it is also clear that Hotman found examples of the Three Estates not only in the Frankish folk assemblies, moreover, were roughly regional in composition. gatherings which, even from his own accounts, suggest purely feudal assemblages to us.[23] The latter oversight is most readily explained by his preoccupation with proving continuity. Feudal assemblies moreover were roughly regional in composition. And Hotman's casual attitude as to the method of selection is all the more understandable when we recall that in the political crisis of his time it was not social class but regional loyalties and confessional affiliation that were the main bases of political alignments.

However this may be, Hotman, it is clear, is generally satisfied that the people as a whole, in the contemporary sense of its politically active segments, was adequately represented in the Estates as they were then composed. His overriding purpose, therefore, is not to reform the composition of the Estates but to restore or revive their political role by reminding his contemporaries of the powers they had anciently possessed. "These," says Hotman, "in brief summation were its powers: first, the power of creating and deposing kings; then, the power of deciding on peace or war, of making public law, of conferring high honors, governorships, and regencies, and of assigning part

---

*The local and regional assemblages in which delegations were chosen were sometimes rather broadly based. (Doucet, *Les Institutions de la France au XVIᵉ siècle*, I, esp. pp. 317-18.) But this should not lead us to believe that Hotman was especially favorable to popular control. Like most writers of his time he expects that elected representatives will be men of substance and responsibility, who will be more moderate than the mass of people generally. He has no objection to the stipulation of the number of representatives to be chosen from the different orders. (See pp. 69-70 below.) The local delegations would thus represent the people as a whole *(populus)* considered as an organized community rather than a collection of individuals. In sixteenth-century usage the mass, or ordinary individuals *(plebeii)*, is only one portion of the *populus.*

It may be noted, however, that here and there proposals explicitly calling for universal suffrage do appear in the period, although these are regularly accompanied by limitations on the nominating process designed to guarantee that respectable persons will be chosen. See, for example, the plan for the local organization of military defense given in *Reveille-Matin des François* (1574), Dialogue I, pp. 143ff. and in Simon Goulart, *Memoires de l'éstat de France sous Charles IX,* Meidelbourg, 1578, Vol. II, pp. 53ff. This scheme, apparently, dates from 1572 and was at least discussed at Millau in 1573 (Goulart, *op. cit.,* II, p. 53). It is reprinted in Haag, *op. cit.,* X, pp. 104ff.

of the domain to the children of a deceased king, or of establishing a dowry for his daughters, which is called an 'appanage' from a German term meaning a part that has been set aside; and, finally, power over all those things which, in the usage of the common people, are called 'affairs of state,' since, as I have said, it was not lawful to take up any part of the commonwealth's affairs except in the council of the Estates or orders."[24]

The powers of the Estates, in this version of the ancient constitution, are thus extended not only to complete control of legislation, but to full supervision of the ordinary conduct of the government. The king could not, for example, alter the established allocation of his incomes, or confer parts of the domain as gifts or appanages, or lay new taxes even in emergencies[25] without the consent of the Estates. And not only fiscal policy but even high affairs of state, including war and peace, the *sanctum sanctorum* of executive prerogative, were reviewed by the Estates each year and subject to determinations that could not be revised in any other place. Crown officials, furthermore, as opposed to mere servants of the royal household, were ultimately responsible not to the king but to the Estates, which had originally elected, or, more properly, appointed them to office, and could, in their judgment, remove them for misconduct.[26] Indeed, the king himself is little more than a responsible executive. He too could be deposed for cause. And "royal majesty" was not a quality inhering in his person but an attribute belonging only to the Estates assembled as a whole, in which the king was but presiding officer.[27] The Estates of old are thus no longer conceived as a consultative body whose consent was required on exceptional occasions, but as the very center of the government. As Hotman puts it ". . . the supreme administration of the kingdom of Francogallia was vested in the annual public council of the nation, which was later called the Assembly of the Three Estates."[28] His description of its power includes almost all those prerogatives of government which his contemporary Jean Bodin listed as the marks of sovereignty.

These ancient rights of the Estates, moreover, are held to be the source of a continuing tradition, and they may be revived against tyrannical perversions without breach of legal continuity. The one important exception, conceded with extreme reluctance, was the transformation of the offices of dukes and counts from elective to hereditary status, a change attributed to Hugh Capet toward the end of the tenth century. This, says Hotman disapprovingly, was "no slight diminution" of the power of the public council. The only reason he assigns for it is the personal ambition of Hugh Capet, who gave certain nobles hereditary rights in office to gain support for his dynastic aims. Nevertheless, his critical examination is abruptly ended with the laconic observation that the change could not have been effected without "the consent of the public council itself," as though he were willing to concede the precedent.[29] He may have felt that vested rights of such long standing should not be attacked,[30] especially since the decrease in the power of the council, although significant, was not decisive. The high officials of the crown, as well as provincial governors, were still appointed. And even hereditary officers could be regarded as responsible to the people rather than the king, since it was the consent of the former that created them.[31]

But where diminution of the rights of the Estates was both more recent and more serious, the demand for restoration is clear and unqualified. The major target here is the Parlement of Paris, which claimed to be the "Senate" of the kingdom and to have sovereign powers of review. This, for Hotman, is a flagrant infringement of the exclusive right of the Estates to supervise the king's administration, and it goes back no further than the fourteenth century. The change, moreover, was intrinsically tyrannical in purpose. It was an attempt of the Capetians to escape supervision by the public council by transferring not only its powers but its ancient name of Parlement to a smaller body whose membership could be controlled. Hence the claims of this "counterfeit Senate" are explicitly branded as a usurpation and dismissed without reserve.[32]

This defense of the Estates was more than academic in its aim. The Parlement of Paris is portrayed as the chief seat of a "judicial kingdom," extending through the provincial Parlements and presidial courts to every part of France. It is savagely attacked by Hotman as the source of that corruption and confusion of French law and procedure which he wished to see reformed and codified.[33] Right below the surface there is perhaps an additional motive for his virulence: the parlements, as guardians of vested interest, had frequently resisted and regularly sabotaged the edicts of toleration for the Huguenots which marked the truces in the civil wars. For Hotman, therefore, the parlements were a major source of the moral corruption that had poisoned France. He obviously looks to the Estates as the effective instrument of radical reform.*

It is sometimes said, however, that Hotman's claim on behalf of the Estates was retracted in the Third Edition, which appeared in 1586. The evidence for this is a newly inserted chapter on existing fundamental laws, the first and most important of which, as might be expected from earlier editions, is that nothing of importance may be done without approval of the public council. But Hotman then observes that the "vestige" of this ancient rule is the power of the Parlement of Paris, whose wide authority is described by the quotation of a solemn passage from Budé.[34] And it is tempting to infer that the sovereign functions of the "Senate" have now been recognized as binding precedent.

It seems to me, however, that this is not an endorsement of the sovereign powers of the Parlement, but rather a temporary waiver of objections. The probable purpose of this chapter of the third edition is to legitimate Huguenot resistance on the basis of existing law. It is the only chapter that is completely new in theme, as well as the only one that deals neither with history nor reflections upon history. Its specific intention, as the title indicates, is to show that despite all changes in the constitution "the king of France is limited," if not by the Estates, then at least by the Parlement of Paris. The concession to the powers of the "Senate" is thus provisional, not positive. Hotman does not say that Senatorial control is a more desir-

---

*The Parlement of Paris, we might note, had also resisted registration of edicts of 1561 embodying many of the reforms proposed in the Estates of 1560. The Estates of 1561 demanded that all decrees executing requests of the Estates of 1560 should be registered by the parlements without modification. See van Dyke, *op. cit.*, p. 492.

able or even equally effective way of securing fundamental law. The Estates, which must still be assembled "as often as public interest demands" and whose powers are still overriding, are in no way debarred from resuming all their rights.* On the contrary, this, it would appear, is what Hotman would in the long run like to see. In the third, as in the earlier editions, the final chapter is devoted to the judicial parliaments with no alteration of the basic message. The usurpation of power by the Senate is recounted exactly as before. The indictment of judicial abuses is not only repeated but augmented.[35]

The *Francogallia* caused an immediate sensation when it appeared in 1573, not only because it was, by contemporary standards, a virtuoso feat of scholarship, but because its political implications were directly relevant. In its most general aspect, the linkage of the rights of the Estates to moral and political reform provided the Huguenot party with an ideology. More specifically, the *Francogallia,* though begun and mostly finished in 1572,[36] already points to the doctrine of resistance to tyrants that was developed by the Huguenots after the St. Bartholomew's Day Massacre later in that year. The rights of the Estates, in Chapter X, are illustrated and confirmed by many parallels from other nations who "have known royal not tyrannical power." [37] This is to show that the right of holding public councils is not an isolated privilege, which a king may casually suppress, but is sanctioned by the *jus gentium,* or common law of peoples, as the nation's sacred right.[38] Chapter XVIII, finally, recounts the resistance of a league of nobles against the tyranny of Louis XI. In Hotman's version, the aim, as well as outcome, of the war was a convocation of the Estates, which was to be the proper remedy for all abuses. The long and pointed narrative is obviously intended to exemplify legitimate resistance. Hotman's account of the procedure in 1467 is substantially the same as the general formula for legitimate resistance presented by Theodore Beza, who was the

---

*Note the apparently deliberate ambiguity of the statement, pp. 91–2 below, in which Hotman explicitly legitimates the veto power of the "Senate" only against the claim of the king to be unlimited, but does not deny that the power of control may properly belong to the Estates.

spiritual leader of the Protestants in France and Calvin's successor at Geneva. We know, indeed, that Beza consulted personally with Hotman, who was at Geneva in the spring of 1573, when Beza's treatise was composed.[39] Hence, Beza's *Right of Magistrates,* which is the first major statement of Huguenot resistance doctrine, may also be considered as a systematic transformation of Hotman's reflections on the ancient constitution into a general constitutionalist doctrine of the state.

The Right of Magistrates

The immediate thesis which Beza sought to validate was relatively new in European thought. For although notions of resistance were deeply rooted in Germanic folk traditions and in the rights of vassals under feudal practice, their theoretical development came much later. The theologians and jurists of the high Middle Ages were much concerned with localist and feudal anarchy and were therefore highly cautious in admitting resistance from below. St. Thomas, for example, excludes resistance on the part of private persons in favor of more regular proceedings, and even so he envisages resistance from below operating against elective monarchies only. The normal remedy, accordingly, is removal of the tyrant from above, in the last instance by the Pope or Emperor. Hence, with certain rare exceptions like John of Salisbury who rehabilitated ancient notions of tyrannicide, a general assertion of the right of resistance to tyrants from below is not encountered until certain of the late scholastics and then only, as we have already pointed out, in a rather abstract and speculative form.

But with the religious conflicts of the sixteenth century, these ideas are rapidly developed. Luther and Calvin, to be sure, are generally opposed to anything but passive disobedience, in the spirit of the early Church. Yet a countercurrent may be noted in their thinking, which was always latent in the Reformation and was to become outspoken among some of their closest friends and associates. The earlier idea. going back perhaps to the Strasbourg reformer, Martin Bucer,[40] is the correction of a ruler by the lesser magistrates, and by 1550 this is stated as a political claim in the *Admonition* of the Lutheran town of Magdeburg against the Interim of the German Emperor, Charles V, in 1548. A king who persecutes the true religion, according to this tract, is no longer a legitimate authority since he was originally established to defend the Law of God. He may be resisted by territorial princes, the magistrates of towns, and other inferior magistrates because they too, insofar as their power is legitimate, have been established to do the will of God.[41] Indeed, at one point in the *Admonition* there is even a hint of the later, constitutionalist rationale. Since the tenure of the lesser magistrates is not affected when the ruler dies, they have an independent power to control him if he should persistently violate God's Law.[42]

Among the Marian exiles, who fled to the Continent from the persecutions under Mary Tudor, the basic idea of the Magdeburg *Admonition* was generalized and made more radical by its association with the idea of a Covenant with God. For Knox, Goodman, and Ponet, every Christian people, like the Jews before them, is obliged by a Covenant with God to defend the true religion. This obligation extends not only to the people's magistrates but, if need be, to every individual. Since each is a "signer" of the Covenant, each is personally responsible to God for the enforcement of its provisions. The power of the people, furthermore, is often confirmed by late scholastic notions of political authority: although God is the ultimate source of all authority, the creation of kings is mediated by the people, who may therefore hold the king responsible and depose him for abuse of his authority.

Thus, by the end of the 1550's almost all the themes of sixteenth-century resistance doctrine had appeared in one form or another. The French development, however, was more systematic and detailed because it was much more deliberate and cautious. One explanation of this caution was the immense authority of Calvin, who would admit resistance by inferior magistrates only where they had a specific constitutional mandate to control the actions of superiors—as did the Spartan ephors, the Roman tribunes, and the Athenian demarchs.[43] Calvin, who was at one time influenced by Bucer, did not

exclude a broader extension of this category. He is willing to
speculate that powers of control may "perhaps" be attributed
to the estates of European kingdoms. And Beza, who was
already Calvin's close associate, approved the Magdeburg
Admonition in a work of 1554 and extended the right of resistance to all inferior magistrates. But in view of their theoretical commitments, neither writer could invoke the rights of
magistrates without full consideration of their competence.

This tendency to caution, furthermore, was surely reenforced
by the precarious position of the Calvinists, not only in France
but also in Switzerland and Germany. Their leaders, here at
least, were extremely careful to avoid or at least disarm the
charge that their religious doctrine was politically subversive.
The Scottish and English reformers could appeal directly to
religious inspiration and were less concerned with legal niceties[44]
because, like the future leaders of the Catholic League, they
represented, or believed they represented, the wishes of the
country as a whole against an isolated tyrant, who had only to
be set aside in one way or another. The Huguenots, however,
were a minority faction facing a protracted struggle and had
to be extremely careful of their grounds if they were to win
over, or at least neutralize, the uncommitted and reassure their
own nobility.[45] Hence, throughout the persecutions of the
1550's, Calvin and Beza consistently urge patience. Both of
them, and especially Beza, showed a certain understanding for
the Amboise Conspiracy of 1560,* but thought it ill-advised.[46]
When they concluded, in 1562, that armed resistance was essential, they preferred the narrowest of grounds, so that the first
religious war was directed not against the king, who was a
minor, but against the Duke of Guise and his associates, who
were alleged to have usurped authority. Even after the St.
Bartholomew's Day Massacre, when confrontation of the king
could no longer be avoided, Beza's justification of resistance
was cautiously and rigorously drawn. This explains why it was

---

*The Amboise Conspiracy was an unsuccessful attempt to seize Francis II, who was a
minor, in order to remove him from what was held to be illegal and tyrannical control
by the House of Guise. The uprising, actually led by a gentleman-adventurer named
La Renaudie, had the secret approval of Louis de Bourbon, Prince of Condé.

to prove more influential and enduring than the work of his Scottish and English predecessors.

The first proposition in Beza's defense of active resistance is that kings are not only established for the welfare of the people but are also created by the people. The proof of this is partly from Scriptural authority, which shows that Jewish kings, although ordained by God, were installed through popular election. It is also proven by the history of famous nations in which procedures of election, or oaths of coronation as the vestige of election, present a uniform pattern of creation by consent. These first two arguments are further confirmed by general reflections on the nature of a people. Since a people, in the thinking of the sixteenth century, was not an aggregate of individuals, but an organized and stratified community, it seemed obvious enough that a people was prior to its king, not only in consideration but in time. As Hotman put it, "a people can exist without a king . . . whereas a king without a people cannot even be imagined." [47] From this it follows that, initially at least, kings were created by the people.

Beza's second proposition is that the creation of a king involved the imposition of definite conditions. Here again there is an appeal to history, sacred and profane, which shows that ceremonies of election and coronation include a promise to obey the law and constitute a kind of compact to which each successive ruler is sworn and bound anew.[48] The existence of this contract, furthermore, may also be confirmed by reason. For if the people is prior to the king and can even get along without him, it has no reason to endow him with authority without establishing conditions to protect its interest. Accordingly, a grant of authority without condition, even were it freely made, would be unreasonable and would not bind.

From these two propositions the general conclusion follows that if a ruler violates the conditions on which authority was granted, the people are no longer obligated and may remove him in favor of another. Historical examples show that peoples of all ages have conceived this as their right. And this is confirmed by analogies from Roman private law.[49] The office of a king may be compared to the office of a guardian, and in all relationships of this description prosecution for abuse of trust is provided under civil law. The obligation of a people to its king is surely not more binding or complete than that of a wife or children to a father, of a freedman to a patron, or of a slave to a master, yet under civil law there are some occasions when even these obligations may be broken. Finally, Beza reenforces these arguments from civil law by appeals to feudal law and canon law as well. The king is like a vassal to his kingdom and forfeits his office for violating faith.[50] Furthermore, the Councils of Basel and Constance have properly decreed that a Church council may depose a Pope.[51]

The remaining and more interesting question, however, is by whom and under what conditions a tyrant may be overthrown. Beza begins by distinguishing two kinds of tyrant: the usurper, from within or from without, who takes power without a legal title; and the ruler who abuses his authority, although his title is otherwise legitimate. The first of these may be opposed by anyone at all, if necessary, since there is no obligation to him whatsoever and he is in the position of a common outlaw. Resistance, indeed, is not only the right of every individual, it is also his sacred obligation, since it is the ultimate means of preserving the community to which he owes his civilized existence. Furthermore, although the original defect of a usurper's title can be overcome by subsequent acknowledgement, the consent must be free and uncoerced and must be understood to bind the ruler to the usual conditions of legitimate authority.

This much of Beza's view on usurpation is but an elegant restatement of a tradition going back to classical doctrines of tyrannicide. But as a theologian, he feels obliged to consider the objection that those who have opposed successful usurpations are condemned by the decree of Providence, on the grounds that ". . . it is God who transfers kingdoms . . . and often gives the victory to tyrants." [52] But the decree of Providence, he argues—or, in more secular language, the unintended consequence of action—does not determine the intrinsic merits of the actions. Although God, who disposes of the outcome, may permit a usurpation to succeed in order to punish a people for

their sins, He neither wills nor approves the intended purpose
of the usurpation, any more than He condemns the intention
to resist, unless of course the decree of Providence is already
specifically revealed. Success, accordingly, does not determine
right or wrong. The fact that God may give the tyrant victory
is cause for penitence and prayer. But it does not affect the
right and obligation to resist.[53]

In justifying resistance to the second class of tyrants, which
is the more decisive and radical conclusion, Beza's position is
more complicated. Unlike his Scottish and English counterparts,
he admits no right of private individuals to initiate resistance
to a tyrant-king. Although he may have been partly moved to
this exclusion by the weight of the Calvinist tradition, his
theoretical grounds are not, at bottom, theological. For if it is
admitted that consent of the people is the proximate basis of
authority, it is possible to argue that every member of the
people has a share of ultimate authority and is not purely a
private subject. But the people, Beza holds, is like a corporate
association whose liabilities to other parties or assets due from
others are discharged or received collectively. On this analogy
from medieval Roman law, which is further elaborated in the
Vindiciae contra tyrannos,[54] the consent to authority, which was
given by the people jointly and collectively, cannot be broken
by a private individual but only by some public process.[55]

But analogies to private law are indecisive in matters of this
sort. It could be argued, for example, that the individual members of a corporation may sue the corporation or its officers
in order to protect their interest. Hence, Beza's particular use
of the analogy is ultimately sustained by considerations specifically political. For "were it otherwise," he says, "infinite troubles would ensue even worse than the tyranny itself, and a
thousand tyrants would arise on the pretext of suppressing
one."[56] The Huguenots, as we have noted, had reason to be
cautious on this question, and we might also add that there
was general concern over the peasant jacqueries and "tumults"
of the urban lower classes which accompanied the civil wars.
Beza's own concern is clear enough from his harsh rejection
of the "Anabaptists," who are identified by writers of the time

with every form of social insurrection. He apparently believed that to admit individual resistance was to give encouragement to such rebellions. His position, therefore, like St. Thomas', is that one must proceed against the tyrant not by private means but by constituted public power.

This power, in the first instance, is the authority of the lower magistrates, which includes all officials, military or civil, feudal or appointive, national or local, who exercise coercive power. These political authorities are the servants not of the king but of the kingdom, or the people. There are not the servants of the king because the tenure of their offices is not affected by his death, and they cannot be removed from office except for cause and by the judgment of a court. But they are the servants of the people since they were originally appointed by the people and take their oaths of office to the kingdom as a whole. By thus combining the concept of the Magdeburg *Admonition* with Hotman's views on the original election of magistrates by the estates, Beza is able to conclude that all inferior magistrates are endowed with "ephoral" authority. They share the king's administration in order to prevent abuses. And they may resort to arms, when necessary, if flagrant tyranny should nonetheless arise. Moreover, although it is officials of the kingdom as a whole whom Beza mainly has in mind, the magistrates of towns and provinces may resist within the confines of their territory. They too, Beza holds without explaining, receive their offices from the kingdom or the sovereignty itself.

The right of the magistrates, however, is, strictly speaking, but the power to constrain. The power to depose is exclusively the right of the Estates, which alone have the sovereign power to apply the ultimate and final remedy of removing the tyrant from his office and establishing a new king in his place.* If the Estates should fail to act, either from obstruction or corruption and if the magistrates connive in this, there is then

*Beza introduces the Estates (p. 113 below) as a third class of "subjects" which is "sometimes" a superior to the king. The usage is peculiar in view of all that he subsequently says about their supremacy. It may be explained either as a vestige of late scholastic usage, or as the influence on Beza of the nomenclature of the *Admonition* of Magdeburg which casts everything in terms of lesser magistrates, or as an awkward way of saying that the Estates are supreme only when assembled.

no further remedy, at least for private individuals, whose sole recourse is prayer or exile. In fact, however, the initiation of resistance by the lesser magistrates can never be precluded (because they can always argue that the Estates have been corrupted or coerced and that a truly free assembly is needed.[57]) Moreover, although Beza is normally thinking of collective resistance by the magistracy as a whole or of a great part of it, resistance by a smaller part is not precluded and is sometimes implicitly envisaged. This means that an opportunity for armed resistance is in practice guaranteed, since it is hard to imagine any sizeable segment of the population, organized to prosecute its grievances, which could not find some prominent magistrate to sound the call to arms.

The power of the Estates to depose is also proven by a lengthy appeal to "the practice of the most famous nations of all ages," since for Beza, as for most contemporaries, deductions from the law of nature, or most general considerations of public utility, seem frail and hypothetical without massive illustration from the *jus gentium,* or common practice. And since the Estates, in this discussion, are regularly equated with the people, the list of illustrations confirms not only the rights of the Estates but also the ultimate power of the people on which the arguments of the preceding sections rest.

In this discussion, Beza's justification for resistance is directly associated with a general principle of constitutionalism. The right of the people to depose a tyrant is not an isolated power but the ultimate guarantee of a set of particular controls upon authority, which are implicit in the act of election. It thus appears, from his discussion of the early Roman kingship, that the "definite conditions" on which the kings of Rome, and all others, were created, included the power of the Senate and the people to make all laws and to supervise administration. The rationale for this is supplied in an extended comment on Samuel's warning to the Jews, which was a celebrated topic in polemics of the time. Samuel's dire picture of how the king, which the people had requested, might behave is not, in Beza's view, a justification of despotic practices, or even a prediction of how kingship must inevitably turn out. It is a warning, rather, against the rule of a single individual, who is likely to slip into tyranny unless he is bridled and constrained. It was the will of God, accordingly, that kings ordained by Him should also be elected by the people so that all should know that they ruled on definite conditions and could also be deposed for violating them. And these definite conditions are clearly intended to include the public rights of the Estates and magistrates.

The content of these rights is left unspecified in many illustrations, presumably for lack of information. But their character for all the cases may be inferred from the detailed exposition of the law of France, which is the illustration that culminates the list, and which is simply a concise summation of the main contents of Hotman's *Francogallia.* The outcome, therefore, is that Hotman's version of the ancient constitution is now fully transformed into a general criterion of political legitimacy sanctioned by the law of peoples. This, in turn, is yet a further argument for the right of Frenchmen to restore their ancient constitution. For Beza, as for Hotman, the ancient constitution had shown its vitality as recently as the reign of Louis XI, and this supports the inference that late subversions are invalid. But along with this appeal to continuity, Beza now asserts that the fundamental rights of Frenchmen, like those of every other people, may not become forfeit through prescription by any law human or divine.[58]

The one remaining question is whether the right to resist may be legimately invoked against persecution of the true religion, on which Beza, once again, is cautious. Like the Scottish and English Calvinists, Beza assumes that protection and enforcement of the true religion is an inherent obligation of the state. Although he does not speak of a covenant with God, it would seem to follow from all that he has said about the constitution that the state's responsibility would fall at least as much upon the people as the king. But this line of argument is simply not explored. The religious obligations of the king are binding on his conscience only. If he should become idolatrous, subjects must be patient in the face of persecution, unless, of course, the right to worship in the true religion has been guaranteed by public law. With Beza, therefore, resistance to religious persecution is cautiously founded on existing public law. Partial toleration had been conceded to the Protestants by the celebrated edict of January, 1562, which Beza himself had helped to draft. The Huguenot resistance is presented in the *Right of Magistrates* as the defense of an established right which has been sanctioned by the country as a whole.

The Vindiciae contra tyrannos

The *Vindiciae contra tyrannos (Defence of Liberty Against Tyrants)*, published in 1579, was probably written in 1574–1575 in its entirety or at least in greater part, by Philippe du Plessis-Mornay, an educated nobleman who was to become one of the chief counsellors of Henry of Navarre after 1576.[59] Mornay's work draws very heavily on Beza's *Right of Magistrates,* and despite certain innovations, its most important contribution is a more ample and eloquent restatement of Beza's major themes. The analogies from feudal and Roman civil law, which are very brief in Beza, are here elaborately explored. The illustrations are not only more numerous but more detailed, and their point is often underlined at length. Beza's outline of the basic constitution is now filled in with subsidiary points of public law. Mornay, finally, is not a theologian seeking to quiet conscientious doubts, but a soldier and a statesman exhorting to revolt, and the style of the *Vindiciae,** accordingly, is more impassioned and rhetorical. Most of Mornay's expansions are matters of detail which need not be considered here. But they are sometimes accompanied by shifts of emphasis that may be briefly summarized.

In the constitutional doctrine of the *Vindiciae* the role of the magistrates is, in comparison, more prominent than that of the Estates, a tendency which reflects the political objectives for which the treatise was composed. The *Vindiciae,* as we have said, is an exhortation to rebel. It invites a military struggle, the initiation and leadership of which inevitably depended

---

*I refer to this work as the *Vindiciae* since this is common usage among historians of political thought. "Defense" or "Defense of Liberty" somehow seem nondescript, and the whole English title is too long for convenient reference.

on the great princes, fighting nobles, and town authorities. Therefore, it makes a special effort to portray these and all other magistrates as the people's guardians with an obligation to defend its rights. At the same time, and even more important, the political goals of this resistance are now more narrowly religious. By 1574–1575, the Huguenots confronted an organized and widespread movement of Catholic militants opposed to toleration and could no longer count upon support from the Estates, at least in the immediate future. Mornay, who was in France throughout this period, must have recognized this fact quite early, for the unfavorable state of public opinion was the ground of his warning to Henry of Navarre against joining in the call for the Estates of Blois in 1576. Political and institutional reform—and therewith the rights of the Estates—is not rejected or disparaged by Mornay. But appeal to the Estates is now regarded, not as the means to a religious settlement, but rather as its consequence and guarantee, once party passions have subsided. For Mornay, therefore, there is no special reason to base his case for the legitimacy of resistance on the rights of the Estates as they once were or ought to be. For his immediate purposes, the more persuasive and effective ground is French law as it actually existed, and he is willing to recognize and even emphasize the supervisory powers of the Parlements and other magistrates where these provide the most convincing proofs of legal limitations on the king.

The consequence of this, however, is a correspondingly diminished emphasis on the role of the Estates. The *Vindiciae* continues to maintain that kings were created by the people, which retains the power to control them. But since convocation of the entire people ultimately proved inconvenient, magistrates were established "to guard the people's rights on an ordinary basis, with the proviso that, should the need arise, the whole people, or an epitome of the whole people, should be convened in extraordinary assembly." [60] Hence, for Mornay, the "magistrates"—in some vague collective sense—may represent the power of the people.* The Estates, no doubt, are still

*The term "represent" or "representation" is extended in the *Vindiciae* to any form of public mandate, and the mandates of officials are broadly construed.

the ultimate authority. But Mornay does not insist on annual or periodic assemblies. Similarly, new legislation and taxation still require the consent of the Estates, or at least, Mornay would qualify, the approval of the Parlement of Paris, as though to suggest that judicial bodies like the French "Senate" or its ancient counterpart, the Jewish Sanhedrin, have a representative capacity in lieu of the Estates.[61] We may note, that, although Mornay, like Hotman, still assumes that the rights of the Estates were once exclusive,* he does not suggest that the acquisition of power by the Senate was a usurpation. The Estates, furthermore, are still an "epitome of the people" and contained deputations elected by the towns or districts.[62] But these deputies are so often equated with the local magistrates —which, of course, they mostly were—that the Estates assembly is sometimes difficult to distinguish from an expanded assemblage of the "magistrates." Finally, although the power to depose a tyrant is still considered the exclusive right of the Estates,[63] the formal act of the Estates is no longer central to the actual description of legitimate resistance. In other words, the demand for an Estates assembly is no longer emphasized as the primary and specific goal of a resistance movement.

In all of this, however, Mornay's intention is not to diminish the rights of the Estates but simply to show that they may, if need be, be represented by the magistrates. On this account the shifts of doctrine with which this substitution is associated turn out to be relatively superficial and unstable. The distinction between Estates and magistrates, as far as powers are concerned, is not so much erased as blurred, since those of the Estates, in principle at least, are overriding. And at the same time the alternative exercise of sovereign powers by the "Senate" or the magistrates is never seriously justified, but simply covered over by the vague assertion that an assembly of the whole people would be awkward, a consideration which would not apply to an Estates assembly. Hence, the one clear point in the *Vindiciae* is that there are authorities independent of the king, established

---

*Except for one very brief remark (p. 00 below), which suggests that the Parlement may have had legislative functions even when it was an itinerant royal council. This very likely is an inadvertent entry of older versions of constitutional history.

in the people's name, which have power to control his every act, and that some or all of these authorities, consulting by any available procedure, formal or informal, may defend the people's rights if the ruler lapses into tyranny. To this extent the constitutionalism of the *Vindiciae* is less an alteration of the doctrine of its predecessors than the transmission of that doctrine without regard for precise jurisdictional relationships. This is the natural result of its greater preoccupation with the immediate justifications of resistance rather than with long-range constitutional reform.

On the same account, however, Mornay is more militant than Beza on the question of resistance on religious grounds. Beza's emphasis on public toleration edicts is not only evasive, as was pointed out, but is not particularly inspiring. The more youthful and ardent Mornay prefers to stand on the overriding religious obligation of the state. On the model of the Scottish and English Calvinists, this obligation is presented as a covenant with God, into which the king and people enter as independent but associated signatories. By an elaborate analogy from Roman law, each is compared to the co-signer of a promissory note, so that each is responsible for the entire obligation in the event of default by the other.[64] The people, therefore, is not only entitled to correct a king who persecutes the true religion. It is obliged to do so since it is responsible for his default. This interpretation of the status of the people as an independent co-partner to the covenant is yet another argument for its general power to control the king. It could not have been accepted in that status if it had surrendered all authority to act.

The *Vindiciae,* furthermore, is somewhat more permissive as to the persons entitled to resist. The burden still falls upon the magistrates, since the exclusion of ordinary private subjects is, if anything, even more scornful and emphatic.[65] The preferred procedure is joint agreement of the "magistrates," here used in the most extended sense.[66] The magistrates, however, are compared to guardians in Roman law. Since the chief guardian is not only supervised by all of the co-guardians conjointly but may, in certain cases, be brought before the courts by any one of them, the officials of the kingdom may act against a tyrant not only collectively but individually.[67] Mornay, therefore, is much more explicit than Beza on the right of general officials to act unilaterally if need be, and he is also more detailed on the right of local magistrates. The covenant with God is binding not only on the people as a whole but also on the units of which it is composed, which are the local subdivisions of the kingdom as opposed to private individuals. The local magistrate, accordingly, is obliged to defend religion in his district if the general officials should default.[68] Furthermore, since the Church is one and indivisible, and each part is responsible for all, it is even hinted that the local magistrate may move beyond his borders. The principle, presumably, is the same as that in Question 4 which deals with intervention by neighboring princes.

It should be pointed out, however, that this emphasis, in Question 2, on the participation of localities in the covenant with God is not to be equated with a federalist conception of the people. Federalism is latent here and there in the *Vindiciae,* but the idea of formation of the people by a contract, real or virtual, is neither stated nor supposed. In Question 3, indeed, which deals with resistance on secular grounds, the local magistrates are, as in Beza, ambiguously described as officers of the kingdom representing particular localities, on which account that they are entitled to resist within the confines of their jurisdiction.[69]

The *Vindiciae,* finally, begins very cautiously but clearly to anticipate resistance by private individuals who have been specially inspired by the call of God. This possibility is discussed by Calvin only with reference to certain cases of resistance in the Bible.[70] Beza mentions special inspiration only to say that he will not discuss it.[71] Mornay, however, boldly says that God, whose mercy is unchanging, may raise up liberators now as in the past. There are many warnings on self-delusions and on the danger of false prophets. Generally speaking, clear external signs should be demanded. But for all of this, the claim of extraordinary calling may also be tested by qualities of mind and conscience.[72] Hence, although roughly the same as that of the *Right of Magistrates,* the resistance doctrine of the *Vindiciae* consistently tends to be more radical.

The three works considered here are only the most outstanding examples of the mass of books and pamphlets that accompanied the Huguenot resistance.[73] The themes of the Huguenots were soon taken over by the Catholic League, especially after 1584, when Henry of Navarre became the heir-apparent. The publicists of the League, indeed, not only repeated but radicalized the doctrine. They often admit individual resistance. They demand political reform and the sovereignty of the Estates as an immediate revolutionary goal. The mendicant preachers, especially, put this doctrine directly to the masses.

Yet among the most remarkable facts about this remarkable constitutionalist agitation is the rapidity with which it all subsided. With the reconversion of Henry of Navarre and his entry into Paris, a religious settlement was rapidly achieved. The Protestants had long been prepared to settle for the version of religious toleration represented by the Edict of Nantes. The majority of Catholics, above all in the upper classes, had rarely been zealous for religious uniformity. The upper strata, furthermore, were disaffected not only by the pro-Spanish leanings of the League, but also by the mass disorders and extended terror that often accompanied the propaganda of its preachers. After 1593 accordingly, these elements, weary of religious war, rallied to Henry IV, whose conversion was sanctioned by the Pope and confirmed by the Gallican Establishment. The zealots of the League were therefore isolated, and the Jesuits were officially expelled.

Thus, with the end of the religious conflict, the constitutionalist movement disappeared as well. Political and institutional reform had always been a secondary goal of the religious parties. The groups of which they were composed were too divergent in their long-range interests to form even the semblance of an opposition party against a determined king who held out the promise of administrative reform. By 1598 the only opposition with which Henry had to deal was the isolated resistance of provincial governors or town authorities trying to maintain the political autonomy they had acquired in the course of civil war.

Despite this political failure, the constitutionalism of this period had a permanent effect on the development of political thought. The ideas that the king was subject to the people or their representatives and that representative bodies were properly supreme are not a mere anticipation of doctrine later to be developed independently, but the source of a continuing tradition. The works of the monarchomachs immediately influenced the political thinking of the Dutch Rebellion. They were frequently used and cited by English writers of the seventeenth century, whose more developed idea of constitutionalism corresponded to more favorable circumstances.[74]

The works which follow have been newly translated from the best available editions. Although all of them are shortened somewhat, every effort has been made to represent their basic form and content. Most of the materials deleted are repetitious examples or analogies, which are of interest mainly to specialists who work in the original language. The deleted matter is almost always summarized or indicated briefly to convey the form and flavor of the original. For the same reason, furthermore, each of the works included is represented in roughly equal proportion to the others. Within each work, all, or almost all, of the main subdivisions are represented. In the *Francogallia* several chapters are summarized, but these are mostly digressions from the theme of the central chapters and are often acknowledged to be such by Hotman.

I should like, finally, to express my gratitude for the generous help that I received. Professor Ralph E. Giesey of the University of Iowa kindly sent me a preliminary version of his variorum edition of the *Francogallia* and offered a number of useful suggestions. The Reverend Jon Gandarias, S. J., who was research assistant in the Department of Political Science at Columbia, was unstinting in his time and interest. Professor Herbert A. Deane read the entire manuscript and made many helpful comments as did Professor Irving Fisher of the University of Maine and Professor Robert J. McShea of Boston

University on the parts of the manuscript they read. My wife, Paula, was not only patient and understanding throughout, but gave me sure editorial advice on the entire manuscript. And I am indebted to Dr. Mark Jupiter of the Columbia University library staff for deciphering and translating the Greek expression on p. 189. Finally, the members of graduate seminars that I have given at Columbia University on various aspects of 16th-century political thought have influenced my thinking in many ways which are difficult to specify. But I should particularly like to mention the stimulation and insight I received from the members of the seminar on constitutionalism which I gave in the fall of 1967 when much of this book was being written. It is a memory I fondly cherish.

Julian H. Franklin
Columbia University
August, 1968

Part I

Francogallia

Editor's Note

François Hotman (1524–1590) came from a family with good connections to the judicial magistracy and may thus be considered upper middle class in background. After an early conversion to Protestantism he was soon accepted into the circle of scholars and theologians that centered on Geneva. At a very early age he became a distinguished professor of law. And like many of the great French jurists of this period he spent most of his career at Swiss or German universities in refuge from religious persecution. After narrowly escaping from the St. Bartholomew's Day Massacre, he left France never to return.[1]

Hotman was a political militant by temperament as well as conviction, and throughout his career he kept in close contact with the Huguenot leadership in France, occasionally performing diplomatic missions for them. Hotman, furthermore, was a formidable pamphleteer. His style, in Latin as well as in French, is lucid and unusually supple. His polemics, written at different times from 1560 to 1585, are masterpieces of the genre in this period. In 1585, finally, Hotman was personally requested by du Plessis-Mornay and Henry of Navarre to defend the claim of the latter as the heir-apparent, and he was subsequently rewarded with a counsellorship. The monograph he wrote, however, is thoroughly consistent with Hotman's intellectual and political commitments, and insinuations of venality are unjust.[2]

Along with these political activities, Hotman was a brilliant teacher and a prolific scholar whose major contributions were in the field of law. He was in fact one of the most celebrated exponents of the new humanist, or "French," method of interpreting the Roman law, in which philological techniques were used to restore the sources of the law and to interpret its meaning in terms of the original usage of words and phrases, and in which rearrangement of the contents was attempted in order to provide a more coherent exposition.[3]

One result of this research, for Hotman as for other humanists, was a growing belief that much of Roman law was irrelevant for understanding European customs, that, as represented in the *Corpus juries*, it was often incomplete and confusing, and that a universal jurisprudence ought to be constructed, drawn from many sources, in which the general virtues and particular problems of European and domestic custom could be given proper weight.[4] Such were the themes that Hotman developed in his *Antitribonian*, composed in 1567, though not published until 1603. His call for a critical understanding of domestic law was generally linked to the idea of political reform. The *Antitribonian* was undertaken at the request of the reformist chancellor, Michel l'Hospital, who was then interested in the codification of French law.

The first fruit of this interest in European customs was the *De feudis commentatio tripertita* of 1572, in which Hotman made extensive use of German terms and origins to clarify the law of fiefs.[5] The second was the *Francogallia,* which was probably begun at the same time as the *De feudis,* when Hotman was teaching at the University of Bourges.[6] But when he fled from Bourges after the St. Bartholomew's Day Massacre, his unfinished manuscript was probably left behind. And the *Francogallia,* which had to be redone at Geneva, did not appear until 1573.

The *Francogallia* was thus one part of an ambitious scholarly enterprise, rather than a *livre de circonstance,* and yet it was, in a very deep sense, inspired by a vision of political reform. Indeed, this union of scholarship with moral and political reform is a fitting motto for Hotman's whole career. The study of ever wider sources was, for him, an attempt to reinvigorate or at least to understand the institutions of the past and those of the present that derived from them.

Hotman's final years were marred by uncertainty and financial hardship. He died at Basel early in 1590.

The *Francogallia* went through two further editions in Hotman's lifetime, each of which was an expansion, rather than an amendment, of the one preceding.[7] Professor Ralph E. Giesey calculates that the original edition represents sixty per cent of the wordage of the final version, half of the remainder having been added in 1576, the rest, in 1586. But the order and structure of the edition of 1573 continued essentially unchanged. Of the seven new chapters added later, only three are really new. Two of these are on actions of the French against the Papacy, one added in 1576, the other in 1586. The third, Chapter XXV of 1586, is a summary of existing fundamental law. The other chapters, most of them dealing with general reflections on the state, are simply subdivisions or expansions of chapters in the previous editions, which are given separate titles in 1586.

Professor Giesey of the University of Iowa will soon publish a variorum edition of the *Francogallia* clearly revealing the successive increments as well as certain alterations of the texts of 1573 and 1576. He will also indicate variations from the final text in the editions of 1599–1600 and 1665 and will provide an exhaustive critical apparatus on Hotman's sources. I am deeply indebted to Prof. Giesey for making this work available to me in preliminary form. It is a model of exacting, devoted, and imaginative scholarship, which will be invaluable to scholars in a number of fields.

The translation that follows is based on the first edition of 1573, since this is the most succinct of Hotman's statements.[8] However, on one or two occasions, where the added documentation of later editions helps to clarify a point of substance, it has been mentioned or quoted in the notes. Chapter XXV of the third edition, which gives Hotman's view of the constitution as it existed in his time, has been included in the form of an appendix.

The bulk of the *Francogallia* deals with the formation of the ancient constitution and its vicissitudes, and all of this material is represented. The other chapters, which are mainly digressions on points of antiquarian interest, are summarized. In all of the chapters represented, the descriptive statements or narrative accounts are amply represented, and where elisions have been made, a summary is almost always given. Many of Hotman's repetitive citations of documents are summarized or only indicated, but a considerable number have been translated intact in order to illustrate the distinctive method of the *Francogallia*. On a rough estimate the translation represents about one-half of the wordage of the first edition.

With the *Francogallia*, unlike the *Right of Magistrates* and the *Vindiciae contra tyrannos*, wherever a reference is translated, the source citation is also included. This is in part because in the *Francogallia* they are included directly in the text and never appended in the margins. But more important it is because Hotman's massive citation of documentary authority is so important to his mode of argument. The inclusion of some of this, accordingly, conveys the special flavor of the work. Almost all of these citations are to obsolete or unavailable editions and, on a few occasions, they are wrong, but there seemed no reason to provide a critical apparatus for present purposes, especially since the task has been carefully performed by Giesey and the results will soon be available in his Latin variorum. I have felt free, however, to alter and correct citations where this did not require alteration of the format of the text or special annotations. References to ancient classics and to certain more familiar Renaissance works have been altered to conform to modern usage and in a few instances have been corrected. The citations to medieval chroniclers have generally been left as is.

Finally, since the sixteenth-century writers do not always indicate quotations clearly, it is sometimes difficult to tell when Hotman is quoting and when he is merely paraphrasing. This difficulty is all the greater since Hotman, who may have often relied solely on his memory, is sometimes very free in his renditions. Giesey, after checking all the references, has made a judgment in each case, which is indicated in his variorum. I have followed his authority in my own indication of direct quotations. Hotman's text, however, has been translated as it stands. And inaccuracies of quotation have not been noted except on one occasion where the error is peculiarly revealing.[9] A closely related problem is that Hotman, in citing medieval chroniclers, is often using editions that have been carried forward in time by continuators who were mostly anonymous. Questions of editions and accuracy of attributions are taken up in Giesey's apparatus, but have not been indicated here.

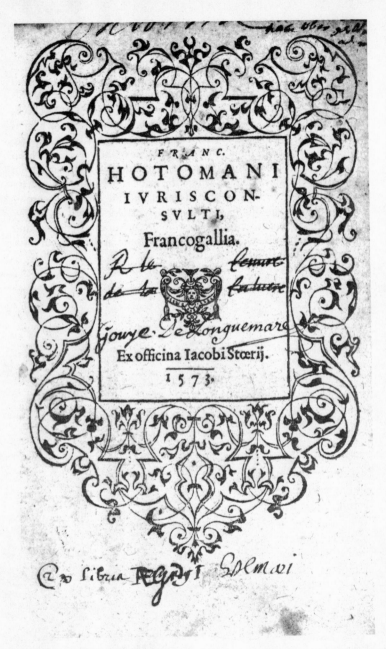

FRANC.

HOTOMANI
IVRISCON-
SVLTI,

Francogallia.

Ex officina Iacobi Stœrij.

1573.

Francogallia

Chapter I

On the constitution of Gaul before it was reduced to a province by the Romans

Since I propose to describe the institutions of our Francogallia insofar as they seem useful to our commonwealth and bear upon our present needs, I think it best to begin by explaining the constitution of Gaul before it was reduced to a province by the Romans. For the origin and antiquity of that people, its military glories, the situation and character of its territory, and its private customs are known to everyone of even modest learning from the extant accounts in Caesar, Polybius, Strabo, Ammianus [Marcellinus], and others.

It should be understood, then, that in the political organization of Gaul at that time, the nation as a whole was not under the government of a single individual and neither the people nor the nobles had exclusive power in the several regions *(civitates).* * Gaul was divided into *civitates,* most of which were governed with the advice of the nobles and were called free, while the rest had kings. But there was one institution to be found in all of them. At a certain time each year they held a public council of the people in which anything that seemed to bear on the general welfare of the commonwealth was settled. Tacitus *(Annales, III)* counts sixty-four *civitates,* meaning regions, as we learn from Caesar, which had not only the same language, customs, and laws, but also similar magistrates, and were like the *civitates* of the Aedui, Arverni, and Rhemi, of which Caesar gives excellent accounts in many places. Thus, when Caesar took steps to have Dumnorix of the Aedui killed,

Civitas literally means citizen-body and refers not only to the region but to its political community.

Dumnorix "prepared to resist and to defend himself," says Caesar, "and he called on his countrymen for support, constantly protesting that he was a free man, and a citizen of a free commonwealth *(civitatis)*." *(De Bello Gallico, V. 7.)* And we find the same judgment in Strabo *(Geog., IV, 4, 3)*. "Most *civitates,*" he says, "were ruled by the advice of the nobles. But in olden times, they chose a single magistrate each year, just as for military purposes, one general was created by the people." In addition, the following comments in Caesar *(VI, 20)* also bear on this: "The *civitates* considered to be best administered are those which have enacted laws that if anyone receives any rumor or information from neighboring peoples, he must report it to the magistrates. The magistrates conceal what they see fit and inform the public of anything they judge will be of use to it. On affairs of state no discussion is allowed except in council."

As to the common council of the entire nation, we may offer these few passages from Caesar. "They asked," he says *(I, 30, 12)* "for permission to call a council of all Gaul for some stated day, and to have Caesar's approval in so doing." Likewise *(VII, 63)*: "A council of all Gaul was called at Bribacte, and a great crowd assembled from every part of the country." And *(VI, 3)*: "Caesar called a council of Gaul to meet in the spring, as was his practice. When the others came, but not the Senones, Carnutes, and Treviri, he transferred the council to Paris." And *(VII, 29)*, referring to Vercingetorix: "He decided to make every effort to rally the *civitates* that dissented from the rest of Gaul and to form a council of all Gaul, which not even the whole world would be able to withstand."

The kings that ruled over some of the *civitates* are mentioned by the same author in almost innumerable passages. And the most important lesson to be learned from these is that it was the custom of the Romans to cultivate any of these minor kings *(regulos)* who seemed suitable for their designs—those, that is, whom they thought could be used to introduce innovations, sow confusion, and foment animosities among the *civitates*. The Romans linked these kings to Rome in league and friendship and passed highly honorific decrees calling them their friends and allies, as though this were the highest of tributes and the greatest of favors. And for these purely verbal honors, a great many distant kings paid heavy bribes to those who ruled at Rome.

"Reges," or rather *"reguli,"* was the term used by the Gauls for rulers who were not chosen for a fixed term like the magistrates of the [free] *civitates* but held permanent royal dominion over any area however small. And it was they who, in the custom of a later age, were called dukes, counts, and marquisses.

Of these *civitates,* furthermore, some were stronger than the rest, and the weaker were eager to become their clients and dependents. Caesar sometimes speaks of these weaker *civitates* as the tributaries and subjects of the stronger. But he most often refers to them as clients. . . .

[The networks of clientage among the *civitates* of Gaul are summarized.]

But there is a noteworthy feature of the kingdoms which ought not to be passed over lightly. In the first place, they were not hereditary but were conferred by the people on those who were reputed just. In the second place, they did not have boundless, absolute, and unchecked power but were bound by settled law, so that they were no less under the people's power and authority than the people were under theirs. These kingships, indeed, seemed to be nothing but magistracies for life. And Caesar gives the names of many private persons whose relatives and ancestors had occupied the throne. Among these is Casticus, the son of Catamantales, whose father had been king of the Sequani for many years *(I, 3);* Piso of the Aquitani *(IV, 12);* and Tasgetius, whose ancestors had been kings of the Carnutes *(V, 25).*

As for the nature of their authority and power, there is a passage in the same author where Ambiorix, king of the Eburones, says *(V, 27)* that "his authority was such that the people had no less power over him than he over the people." And this is the form of commonwealth that is rated best and most excellent by Plato, Aristotle, Polybius, and Cicero. For, as Plato says, if royal government is left without a bridle, it obtains so much power over everything that it stands, as it were, on slippery ground and very easily falls into tyranny; for which reason it should be bridled and constrained by the authority of the nobles and selected men who are entrusted with this power by the people.*

Chapters II–V

[In Chapter II, Hotman refutes a fairly widespread opinion that the ancient Gauls spoke Greek. He agrees with Beatus Rhenanus that the language used in certain parts of Brittany is a remnant of the ancient language. He concludes that the French language of his day comes half from Latin and half—in roughly equal proportions—from the Franks, the ancient Gauls, and the Greeks (via Marseilles).

In Chapter III, Hotman describes the subjugation of the Gauls and the oppressive burden of the Roman yoke. But prior to the conquest, the Gauls were held in awe throughout the civilized world as a result of their military exploits.

Chapters IV and V are erudite discussions of the origins of the Franks and of their gradual movement into Gaul. The Franks, whose name means freemen, were a Germanic tribe situated near the sea between the Rhine and the Elbe who spread beyond their borders in defiance of Roman power. When they appeared in Gaul, they came as liberators and were welcomed by the Gallic population. The outcome of their migrations was thus a new nation created by the fusion of the Franks and Gauls. Strictly speaking, the first king of the French was not Pharamond or Merovée, who were kings only of the Franks, but Childeric, who was truly king of the Francogalli, or the French.

"For although some take Pharamond and Clodio as the first kings of France, there were surely many Frankish kings before them who crossed the Rhine and made incursions into Gaul

*Refers generally to Plato's warnings against despotic monarchy in Laws, III, which is a favorite reference for writers in this period. See, for example, Laws, III, 693.

without being able to establish a settled dominion within its borders. Merovée, who is commonly taken as the third king, was actually king in France, yet he was a stranger and a foreigner, was not made king in Gaul, and was not elected by the Francogalli—that is, by the judgment and decree of the public council of the combined and associated nation. In short, all of the above were kings of the Franks, not of the Francogalli, whereas Childeric was the first to be elected by the Franks and Gauls in a public council of the united people."]

Chapter VI

Whether the kingdom of Francogallia was conveyed by inheritance or by election, and on its manner of creating kings

But at this point an important question arises which will also reveal the wisdom of our ancestors—was the kingdom of Francogallia conveyed by hereditary right or by the judgment and votes of the people?

Our Franks, it has been shown, were a Germanic people, and German kings used to be created by the ballot, as Tacitus indicates in his book on the customs of the Germans. "They choose their kings for nobility," he says *(Germania, 7)*, "and their generals for valor." The Germans, the Danes, the Swedes, and the Poles still retain this institution, and elect their kings in the council of the nation, although the sons [of a deceased king] enjoy a privileged position and (as Tacitus reported) are preferred to others.

No institution wiser than this or more salutary for a commonwealth could, in my opinion, be conceived. For as Plutarch nicely puts it in his life of Sulla [and Lysander], just as hunters do not ask for the offspring of a spirited dog, but for a dog that is spirited himself; and as horsemen do not ask for the offspring of a spirited horse, but a horse that is spirited himself; so those who are organizing a commonwealth are much mistaken if they choose their prince by accident of birth rather than by proven merit.

And that this was the wise intention of our ancestors in establishing the kingdom of Francogallia is documented, to begin with, by the testatment of Charlemagne, as published by Johannes Nauclerus and edited by Henricus Mutius, in which the following clause appears: "If a son is born to any of my three sons and the people wish to elect him, let him succeed his father as heir to the kingdom; and it is our will that his uncles should consent and should permit their brother's son to take his father's portion of the kingdom." And similarly the following passage in Aimon *(I, 4),* on Pharamond, who, as I have said, is commonly taken as the first king of France: "The Franks, electing a king in the manner of the other nations, raised Pharamond to the royal throne."

[There follows additional documentation from medieval chroniclers including Gregory of Tours, Ekkehart, Luitprand of Cremona, Sigebert, and Otto of Freising.]

From these passages and many others like them, I think it is clear that the kings of Francogallia were constituted by the people and not by hereditary right. And another weighty argument for this is the ceremony used by our forefathers for inaugurating kings. As we said a little earlier, Tacitus indicates that the Caninefates, a Frankish people, placed the king-designate upon a shield and carried him high upon their shoulders, and we have noted that the same was done with our kings. Whoever had been chosen by the people was lifted to men's shoulders, seated on a shield, and carried three times around the assembly of the people or the army, while everyone applauded and shouted their approval. . . .

[Documentation is supplied from Gregory of Tours, Aimon, and Ado of Vienna.]

And now we must proceed to the third part of this argument, which is to understand how great the right and power of the people was, not only in creating kings but in retaining them, since it is evident from all our chronicles that the supreme power of deposing kings resided in the people. Striking documentation of this power is provided for us by the fate of the first man to be created king of Francogallia. When the people discovered that he was devoted to vices and to lust and spent his time with bawds and prostitutes, they removed him by public agreement and forced him to get out of Gaul. And our chroniclers attest that this happened in 469. And when Eudes, the man with whom they filled his place, abused his power also and became arrogant and cruel, he was judged with equal severity and stripped of his authority. . . .

And this glorious and remarkable deed of our forefathers is all the more carefully to be noted in that it came at the beginning and, as it were, in the childhood of the kingdom, as though it were a declaration and announcement that they created kings in Francogallia, subject to specific laws, and did not establish tyrants, with powers absolute, unlimited, and free. . . .

[Six more examples are advanced, the most recent of which deals with Charles the Simple in 926. These and the preceding cases are variously drawn from Gregory of Tours, Aimon, Godfrey of Viterbo, Sigebert, Ekkehart, and Otto of Freising.]

Chapter VII

The rule of inheritance when there was more than one survivor of a deceased king

The preceding seems to show that in ancient times the kingdom of Francogallia used to be conveyed not by right of inheritance, as though it were a private legacy, but by the judgment and votes of the people. Therefore, there is not much point in asking about the rule that was followed in determining the rights of the children of a deceased king. For, since the assembly of the people and public council of the nation had supreme power not only to confer the kingdom but withdraw it, it necessarily follows that the same body decided whether to confer succession to the kingdom on all children equally or on only one.

There is another question here, however. If the people rejected the king's son and elected someone else, was anything left to the son in order to maintain his dignity? To answer this we have to understand that the possessions that are subject to the king's control are divided into four classes by the jurists: the possessions of Caesar (as they say), the possessions of the treasury, public possessions, and private possessions. The possessions of Caesar refer to the private patrimony of the individual prince, not insofar as he is prince, but insofar as he is Louis, Lothaire, or Dagobert. Under French law, furthermore, this patrimony is called "the property of the king" and cannot be alienated without approval by the public council of the nation, as will be seen a little later on when we discuss the council's authority. The possessions of the fisc are what the people have voluntarily given to the king, partly to maintain his dignity and partly for unexpected public expenses. What the jurists call "public possessions" are the property of the kingdom and commonwealth as such, while "private possessions" refer to the wealth and resources of all the fathers of a family. Therefore, if a king dies and the inheritance of the kingdom is conferred upon a stranger, possessions that are properly the king's and are, as the jurists say, his patrimonial inheritance, and which we have said cannot be alienated by him, are left to his children by right of inheritance. The possessions of the kingdom and commonwealth, however, since they are a part of the kingdom, must necessarily devolve to him to whom the kingdom goes, although reason dictates that duchies and counties should be assigned to the children [of the deceased king] by the people's assembly for the purpose of maintaining their dignity.* . . .

Now to return to our initial question on succession to the kingdom. I find no clear-cut rule on this in Francogallia since it was not, as I have said, hereditary. As to the other noble inheritances, which are known as fiefs, Otto of Freising says

*This cryptic account of royal fiscal rights is expanded at great length in the third edition. For a rough parallel to this later treatment, see below, p. 174ff.

(Gesta Frederici Imperatoris, II, 29): "The custom in Burgundy, which is observed in almost all the provinces of France, is that control of the paternal inheritance always passes to the older brother, or to his children male or female, the remaining brothers looking on him as their lord." . . . But on succession to the kingdom the law was different. For the records show that in ancient times the kingdom of Francogallia was often not given by the people to one of the sons at the death of a king but was divided into male portions and distributed. . . . On the other hand, Otto of Freising *(Chronicon, V, 9)* and Godfrey of Viterbo write that, around 630, after the death of Lothaire, the seventh king, "Dagobert, the son of Clothaire II, was the sole ruler in France, but he had given his brother Heribert a few towns and villages near the Loire. Before this the kingdom of the Franks, from Clovis on, had been variously divided among the king's sons, and the sons of his sons, and was ruled with much confusion. And the borders of the Frankish kingdom now stretched from Spain to Hungary, and so Dagobert, the sole king of the Franks, gave laws to the Bavarians." So writes Godfrey, and not unjustly, as many experts have remarked. For, as Justin says *(XXI, 1, 2),* "If a kingdom is kept in the hands of a single individual, it will be more stable than if it is apportioned among several brothers."

Nevertheless, a few years later at the death of the Pippin, with the Frankish kingdom extended far and wide, the public council of the French was pleased to choose the other course, which serves to confirm what we said above, namely, that all legal claims in this area lay in the discretion of the council. For Einhard in his *Life of Charlemagne* says, "At the death of Pippin, the Franks, in general assembly, solemnly decided to make both his sons kings, on condition that they would share the whole body of the kingdom equally, and that Charles would assume responsibility for ruling the part their father Pippin held, Carloman, his uncle's portion." . . .

It is thus very clear from this investigation that in ancient times there was no definite rule on this subject in Francogallia amd that full power in this area rested with the public council of the nation. It is true that later on, at the initiative of Philip

III, the forty-first king, it was decided that some sort of estate should be provided for younger brothers, but there were varying interpretations of this rule also, and many controversies on the position of daughters, so that it is clearly impossible for us to render any definite opinion on the subject except to say that were we to return to the ancient procedure of our forefathers, the determination of all claims in this domain ought to be entrusted to the public council of the nation, which would assign estates to each of the king's children to be used for their needs and their refinements.

Chapter VIII

On the Salic law and the right of women in royal inheritances

Since we have started to discuss the law of royal inheritance, we must not fail to mention the Salic law, which not only is a favorite topic in our day, but which, within the memory of our forebears, once served to settle a great and dangerous dispute over succession to the throne. In 1328 King Charles the Fair, a son of Philip the Fair, left a pregnant wife as he lay dying, and a few months later a daughter was born. King Edward of England, the son of Isabella, who was Philip the Fair's daughter and King Charles' sister, contended that the inheritance of his grandfather's kingdom belonged to him. On the other side, Philip of Valois, son of the brother of King Charles the Fair's father, rose in opposition, claiming that there was an ancient fundamental law *(legem regiam),* called the Salic law, which excluded women from inheriting the kingdom. Gaguin and other writers of that sort claim that this law was written by Pharamond, and that it continued to be "very well-known up to our own times." And in his life of Philip of Valois he says, "Edward was excluded by the Salic law which was given to the Franks by Pharamond and had been very scrupulously observed up to Edward's time. Under this law, only royal descendants of the male sex governed the kingdom, and females were not admitted to that dignity. The phrasing of the law is as follows. 'No portion of inheritance of Salic land shall pass to a woman.' Salic land, in the usage of French jurists, is the king's land only and is different from allodial land, which extends to subjects also to whom this law gives free ownership of some valuable right, not excluding the prince's majesty." This opinion has been shared until now not only by every French historian, but even by the jurists and advocates, as may be documented from Papon *(Arrests, IV, 1),* so that by now the error has pretty much created law.

Nevertheless, we should recall, as was pointed out above, that the Franks had two centers, and two kingdoms. One of these was in France and has continued to this day; the other was across the Rhine near the Saal River, so that the Franks there were called either Salian or Salic Franks, but most often and more precisely, Salici; and their kingdom, and their very name, almost, now has passed away. Remarks on the Salians in Ammianus Marcellinus' history were given earlier, and it was shown that they were called Eastern, and the others were called Western, Franks. Moreover, just as there were two Frankish kingdoms, so there were two Frankish laws: the Salic for the Salians, and the Frankish, for the Francogalli. . . . [Einhard, the preface to the Salic law, Otto of Freising, and Sigebert are cited to show that the Salic law was the law of the Salian Franks.] And these are the words of our ancient chroniclers from which we may expose the error of those who have derived "Salic" law from *"sal"* (salt) and would then render it as "prudent saying," or who have traced it to a corrupt pronunciation of *"Gallica"* (Gallic), than which nothing could be more absurd.

But much greater errors have sprung from the same source. First, there is the belief, supported by authors like Gaguin, that the Salic law relates to the public law of the commonwealth and state and establishes hereditary succession to the throne. But the texts of the Salic law were found not many years ago and have been published; and, first, we discover from the writing, that they were written and promulgated around the time of King Pharamond, and, second, we can also see that all the articles, both of the Salic and the Frankish law, dealt only with private law, not with the public law of the commonwealth and state. Among them, furthermore, there is this article in title 62: *"No portion of inheritance in Salic land goes to a woman, but the male sex acquires it,* that is, the sons succeed to the inheritance. *But if, after a long time, a dispute on the portion should arise among grandsons or great-grandsons, let it be divided not by branches, but by heads."* A law similar to this is to be found in the *Law of the Ripuarian* [Franks], title 58. And so also in the *Law of the Angles,* title 7, all of which are so far removed from legislating on royal inheritances that they do not even deal with fiefs, but only with allodial inheritances, [which were always male] although dowries for women were assigned from them.

But however this may be, this much is clear. Even if there is no provision either in the Salic or the Frankish law by which women are excluded from inheriting the kingdom, the practices and customs of the nation preserved with such complete agreement over centuries obtain the force of written law. Thus at the death of Childeric, the third king, who left two surviving daughters, the kingdom was conferred upon his brother Clothaire while the daughters were excluded. Again, when Cheribert, the fifth king died, with three surviving daughters, succession was conferred on his brother Sigebert. Similarly, at the death of Gontran, king of Burgundy and Orleans, the kingdom was not given to Clotilda, his sister, but to his brother, Sigebert.

Furthermore, the counsellors of Philip of Valois would have shown much more judgment and prudence if they had based their argument on feudal law under which the inheritance of fiefs is conferred only on offspring of the male sex, and women are not admitted. Moreover, where the branch in which a fief is vested becomes devoid of males, the fief is transferred to another branch, which is what happened in that case. And those fiefs which, by distortion of the law, are conferred on women, are not, properly speaking, fiefs *(feuda)* but should rather be called *feudastra,* as we have shown in other writings.*

*A reference to his *De feudis commentatio tripertita.*

[Chapter IX deals with the custom, among early French kings, of wearing their hair long. This style, it is argued, was common to all Gauls and Franks before it became a royal privilege.]

Chapter X

The form in which the kingdom of Francogallia was constituted

Now that these matters have been briefly taken up, we should next explain the form in which the kingdom of Francogallia was constituted. We have already shown that the people reserved to itself supreme power not only to make but also to remove a king. This is clearly the form of rule that our Gauls had before they were subjected to the power of the Romans, since the people, as Caesar says, had no less dominion and power over the king than the king had over the people. But it is likely that our Franks derived this form of constitution not from the Gauls but from their fellow Germans, of whom Tacitus, in his book on the customs of the Germans *(7)*, writes: "The power of their kings was not unlimited and free."

And no form [of government] is more remote from tyranny than this. Indeed, of the three marks of tyranny noted by the ancient philosophers, not one is to be found in the constitution of our kingdom. First, as to forced obedience—that is, where the king is a ruler of unwilling subjects—we have already shown that the supreme power of both choosing and deposing kings lay in the people. As to foreign bodyguards, which they mention as the second mark of tyranny, the kings of Francogallia, far from using foreign and alien mercenaries as a palace regiment, did not even have a bodyguard of citizens and native-born, since assurance of protection was wholly placed in the fidelity and love of their followers. . . . The third mark of tyranny is that everything is decided according to the will and

convenience of the ruler, not of the commonwealth and subjects, and we will show a little later on that supreme administration of the kingdom of Francogallia was vested in the annual
public council of the nation, which was later called the Assembly of the Three Estates.*

The constitution of this kingdom then is the one which the
ancient philosophers—including Plato and Aristotle, whom
Polybius followed—declared to be the best and most excellent,
a constitution, namely, which is a blend and mixture of all
three simple types: the royal, the aristocratic, and the popular;
which is the form of commonwealth that Cicero rated above
all the others in his *On the Commonwealth.* For since royal and
popular dominion are antithetical by nature, a third component
should be introduced which is between them and common to
them both, and this is the nobility, or leading men, who approach royal dignity by the antiquity and splendor of their race
and yet, because of their vassalage or, more colloquially, subjection, are not too distant from the commoners. For, together with the commoners, they acknowledge one and the
same person as magistrate of the entire people. This noble
moderation in a commonwealth has been praised by Cicero
in a striking passage based on Plato's *Republic,* and because
of its unusual elegance we shall repeat it here. "With lutes and

---

*Added in subsequent editions: Claude Seyssel, in the book he wrote on *Monarchie de
France,* finds the explanation of this name in the three orders [estates] of citizens.
and assigns the highest status to the nobility, the intermediate to the judges and merchants, and the lowest to artisans and farmers. He says in I, 13: 'In this kingdom we
have a form of commonwealth which should be greatly praised and jealously preserved,
since it is very effective in maintaining concord among the orders. And there is no
doubt that, so long as each order is guaranteed its right and dignity, it is difficult to
shake the kingdom. For each order has its own privilege, and if this is preserved, no
one of them can overthrow another, nor can all three conspire against the prince and
monarchy simultaneously. I do not include the clergy as one of these estates because
it is mixed among all three. I classify the three estates or orders as follows—first, the
nobility, then the middle people who may be called the wealthy, and last, the lowest,
and commoners.'

But since the tripartite scheme in question relates not to the order of communal life
but to the public council of the nation (which is why that council is popularly called
the Three Estates), let us see whether its name cannot be more conveniently attributed
to the three elements *(genera)* of which that council is composed—*i.e.,* the royal, the
aristocratic, and the popular.

pipes, and with singing and voices a certain adjustment of distinct sounds is needed which, if altered or discordant, is unbearable to trained ears; and this attunement, achieved by the moderation of very dissimilar voices, creates harmony and congruence. Similarly, the highest, lowest and intermediate orders of a commonwealth join, like sounds, in a consensus of highly dissimilar elements, when the principle of moderation is applied. And what musicians call harmony in singing is called concord in a commonwealth, and it is the best and strongest bond of safety, which, without justice, cannot possibly exist." *(On the Commonwealth, II, xlii, 69)*.

This tempered mixture of three elements is, thus, the commonwealth adopted by our forefathers, and they wisely decreed that a public council of the entire kingdom should be held each year on the first of May, in which council all the major business of the commonwealth would be settled by the common counsel of all of the Estates. And the wisdom and usefulness of this institution can be seen mainly in these three considerations: First, there is much wisdom in a large number of experienced men, as Solomon and other sages have observed. Secondly, it is an essential part of liberty, that affairs should be administered by the advice and authority of those who have to bear the risk, as in the common saying that "what concerns all should be approved by all." And finally, those who have great influence with the king and hold great offices can be kept within the bounds of duty through fear of that council in which the remonstrations of the provinces *(civitatum)* are freely voiced. For, as Aristotle very rightly observes in his *Politics (III),* kingdoms governed at the discretion and pleasure of the king alone are not governments of men who are free and have the light of reason, but rather of sheep and brute beasts who have no judgment. Moreover, just as sheep are not ruled by one of their own species, and boys or adolescents are ruled not by one of their own peers but by a superior, so a multitude of men should be ruled and governed, not by some one individual among them, who may be among the least discerning of their number, but by men approved and selected by the consent of everyone as being more eminent;

and by mutual counsels; and by one mind compounded out of many, as it were.*

Now insofar as most kings have an ordinary privy council whose advice they prefer to take in administering the commonwealth, we should say, in the first place, that it is one thing to be a councillor of the king, another to be a councillor of the kingdom. Furthermore, these privy councillors *(Senatores assidui)* either remain in one place or constantly attend the prince's court and can have no knowledge of outlying provinces nor readily grasp their condition. Besides, once they are initiated into the luxury of the royal palace, they are easily corrupted by love of domination, ambition, and avidity, so that in the end they are no longer councillors of the kingdom, but the king's own private flatterers and ministers to the king's vices together with their own. And on this there is a striking saying by the Emperor Aurelian reported by Flavius Vopiscus *(Aurelian, XLIII)*, "I heard from my father," says Aurelian, "that, when he was still a private citizen, the Emperor Diocletian said that nothing was more difficult than to rule well. Four or five men get together; they agree upon a plan to deceive the emperor; and they tell him what to do. The emperor, who is locked up in his palace, does not know the truth; he knows only what they tell him. He makes judges of persons who should not be judges. He turns persons out of public service whom he ought to have retained. And how much else? As Diocletian used to say, the good, careful, and virtuous emperor is thus betrayed."

Therefore, when our forefathers formed our commonwealth, they steered clear of reefs like these and decreed that the commonwealth should be directed by the common counsel of all Estates and that to provide this consultation the king, the nobles, and the delegates from the several provinces should hold an assembly at a fixed time each year. And we may observe that the same institution was adopted by many other nations also. Thus, we have shown above that our ancient Gaul was administered by a common counsel of elected deputies. And, since we are now talking about kingdoms, it is clear

*A vague reference to *Politics, III, XI.*

enough that, in ancient Greece, as Suidas and others attest, the Amphyctionic Council was instituted by King Amphyction, the son of Deucalion, so that at a certain time of the year deputies from twelve Greek cities assembled at Thermopylae and, in common consultation, deliberated on the main affairs of the kingdom and the commonwealth. For this reason Cicero calls it the "common," Pliny the "public council of Greece."

It is evident that the Germans showed the same wisdom in organizing the German Empire, in which the Emperor represents the monarchical element, the princes, the aristocratic, and the delegates of the provinces, the democratic; and where nothing bearing on high affairs of the German commonwealth is considered firmly settled unless it has been ratified in the assembly of these three estates. Also related to this, is that old and famous institution of the Spartans, which established the Ephors, who were to be bridles on the kings, as Plato writes, and by whose advice and authorization the kings were to administer the commonwealth. Pliny *(Nat. Hist., VI, XXIV, 90)* records the same arrangement on the island of Ceylon, where the king was assigned thirty governors by the people, whom he was to consult in administering the commonwealth so that he would not have unlimited power over his fellow citizens and put them on the same level as his slaves or sheep.

That the same form of government is to be found among the English also is documented by Polydore Vergil, in *Historiae Anglicae (11),* where he writes: "Prior to these times (he is describing the life of Henry I), kings normally called an assembly of the people for purposes of consultation only upon rare occasion, so that it may be justly said that this institution came from Henry. And it has always been so deeply rooted, now as well as then, that from that time on all deliberations on the right management and preservation of the commonwealth were transferred to that council. And any act or decree that had been passed by order of the king or of the people was held to be completely void until it had been confirmed by the council's authority. And to free the council from the opinions of the ignorant crowd, which is characteristically devoid of wisdom, there was, from the beginning, a law specifically determining which priests and which, as well as how many, of the rest of the people should be summoned to the council. In the French manner, this council is commonly called a "Parliament," and each king customarily holds one at the beginning of reign and thereafter summons it at his discretion whenever necessary."

But of all these institutions of almost all the nations none is as remarkable as the Spanish. When the Spanish create a king in the common council of Aragon, they commemorate the event by enacting a play. They bring in a man whom they name the Justice of Aragon, and by a public decree of the people they solemnly declare that he is greater and more powerful than the king. Finally, the king, who is created subject to definite laws and conditions, is addressed in these words, which we reproduce here because of the outstanding and exceptional firmness of that people in putting a bridle on their king. *"Nos qui valemos tanto come vos, y podemos mas que vos, vos eligimos rey, con estas y estas conditiones: intra vos y nos, un que manda mas que vos."* That is, "We who count as much as you, and can do more than you, elect you king on these and these conditions: between you and us there is one who has more authority than you."*

In view of all of this, and since this, I say, has always been the practice of all peoples and nations that have known royal and not tyrannical power, it is completely evident that this splendid liberty of holding public councils is part of the common law of peoples, and that kings who scheme to suppress this scared liberty are violators of the law of peoples and enemies of human society, and are to be regarded not as kings but tyrants.

But let us return now to our initial line of inquiry. Since the form of our commonwealth, as it was constituted by our ancestors, was, as we have shown above, a mixture of the three main kinds of state, it was ordained that a public council should be solemnly convened each year and also whenever any great event occurred. And this council is called the "Parliament of the Three Estates" since the term *"parlamentum"* designates a conference and assembly of men coming together from a

---

*At this point the third edition introduces a very long list of quotations, from numerous sources, on the office of the *Justicia* of Aragon.

variety of places to deliberate on common concerns; and so, for example, conferences between enemies to arrange a peace or truce are always called *"parlamenta"* in our chronicles.

In this Parliament the king presided seated on a golden throne around which sat the princes and the magistrates of the kingdom and below them the delegates of the several provinces, who in popular usage are called "deputies." On the day of the meeting the king was escorted to the chamber in a public procession that had greater resemblance to popular modesty than to royal pomp. And although the court sycophants of this degenerate age will surely break into laughter, we shall reconstruct this ceremony from our ancient records, since it is the part of piety to rejoice in the wisdom of one's forefathers. The king, then, was taken to the chamber in a wagon drawn by oxen, which were driven by a simple cartman with his goad. When they arrived at the chamber or, rather, the temple of the commonwealth, the princes conducted the king to his golden throne, and the rest, as has been said, took seats according to their place and rank. And it was this arrangement and this temple with which royal majesty used to be identified, a striking reminder of which may be noted in the royal emblem that is commonly called the "Chancellor's Seal." The king is not depicted mounted on a military charger or riding in a triumphal chariot, but robed and crowned, seated on his throne holding the royal sceptre in his right hand and the sceptre of justice in his left, and presiding in a solemn council. Thus, it is profoundly true that the term "royal majesty" correctly and properly applies only to a consultation on great affairs of state, and that it is an ignorant and vulgar corruption of the term to use the term royal majesty on all occasions, even when the king is at play, or dancing, or chatting with young girls.

On all these matters we shall select only a few of very many documents. . . . [The use of an ox-cart by early kings and the throne ceremonial are documented at length from the chroniclers.]

Now as to the authority of the members of that council, we have this documentation from Aimon *(IV, 4)* where he is speaking about Clovis II. "Fellow Franks," says Clovis, ". . . the duties of our earthly dominion require us to call you together to consult on public matters." So also in the same book *(74):* "At the beginning of the summer he entered Saxony and held an annual general assembly there, as he used to do each year in France." Likewise, *IV, 13,* where he speaks of Charlemagne: "After the hunt at Aix-la-Chapelle was over, he came back and held a solemn general assembly of his people." . . . [Three more quotations from Aimon follow.]

The preceding quotations refer to that solemn council which both French and German historians, using a corrupt form of Latin, sometimes called "the court" *(curia),* sometimes "general assembly" *(conventus generalis),* but most often *"placitum."* Thus, Gregory of Tours *(VII, 14):* "Therefore, as the date of the *placitum* approached, they were directed by King Childebert, and so on." Aimon *(IV, 109)* says: "In the middle of the month he held a general assembly at Thionville which was attended by a great multitude of Franks." Then, a few lines later he adds: "Conspicuous in this *placitum* was the exceptional mercy of this very pious emperor." And it was the custom then to send gifts to the king from every part of the kingdom which were presented to him in the council, as is recorded in many other places where that council is called the "general assembly." Thus Aimon, in *IV, 64,* where he is speaking of King Pippin: "He forced them to promise that they would do everything he wished, and that every year, as a mark of respect, they would send a contribution of 300 horses to the general assembly." So also *(85):* "Recalling the Saxons' perfidy, he called a general assembly in the traditional manner to meet at Kostheim across the Rhine."

But this council was also called "the court" *(curia),* whence the expression of the common people, who say of someone travelling to the king's residence that he is going to the court, because the common people are rarely near the king unless there has been a council called on affairs of great importance. Also Aimon, *(V, 50):* "Charles, son of the Danish king, brought an action in the *curia* against certain Flemish noblemen." Likewise, in the following chapter: "At the death of Henry, King of the Romans, in the great general court *(curia)* held at Mayence. . . ." [A similar instance of this terminology is quoted from Otto of Freising.]

Chapter XI

On the inviolable authority of the public council and the kinds of things decided there

We have now reached the point where we may consider the kinds of things decided in the public council and admire the wisdom of our ancestors in ordering our commonwealth. These, in brief summation, were its powers: First, the power of creating or deposing kings; then, the power of deciding on peace and war, of making public law, of conferring high honors, governorships, and regencies, and of assigning part of the domain to the children of a deceased king or of establishing a dowry for his daughters, which is called an "appanage" from a German term meaning a part that has been set aside; and, finally, power over all those things that, in the usage of the common people, are called "affairs of state," since, as I have said, it was not lawful to take up any part of the commonwealth's affairs except in the council of estates or orders.

As to the power of creating or deposing kings, we have advanced sufficient evidence above, from Charlemagne's testament as well as from other authors. Nevertheless, we should not pass over this one additional quotation, which is from Aimon, *(V, 17)*, where he is speaking about Charles the Bald. "At a general assembly held at Crécy," says Aimon, "he presented his son Charles with his manly armor, that is, girded him with sword; placed the royal crown upon his head; and assigned him Neustria, and Pippin, Aquitania."

As to regencies of the kingdom, we have the following evidence from the same author, writing about the same Charles the Bald *(V, 35):* "Charles, leaving for Rome, held a general assembly on the first of June at Compiègne where, in a number of articles, he prescribed how his son Louis, together with his vassals and the notables of the kingdom, were to rule France until Charles returned from Rome." Likewise, in the same book, *42,* where he is speaking of Charles the Simple: "In view of his age, the notables of France judged him un-

suited to exercise dominion, as indeed he was, and so the leading men of France, Burgundy, and Aquitaine met together
to elect Odo as Charles' tutor and governor of the kingdom."

And as to laws and ordinances this one passage in Gaguin's
life of St. Louis *(De Francorum regum gestis)* is sufficient documentation: "When he returned to Paris, Louis, having called a
general assembly, reformed the commonwealth, making excellent laws on judicial procedure and prohibiting the sale of
offices, etc."

As to the conferment of high honors and governorships on
upright men, there is evidence in Aimon *(V, 36),* where he
speaks of Charles the Bald. Since Charles, prior to his inaugura-
tion, had assigned governorships of the kingdom at his own
discretion, the notables called a solemn council, sent ambassadors to the king, and would not permit him to be crowned
until he recognized their council and accepted its authority in
commissioning the magistrates in question. "The notables of the
kingdom," says Aimon, "were indignant, because he had given
honors to certain men without their consent, and on account
of this they conspired against him, and they convoked their
own assembly in the town of Witmar and from there sent ambassadors to Louis, who in turn sent ambassadors to them," etc.
Similarly, Gregory of Tours, *(Appendix, XI, 54):* "That year
Clothair met with the leading men and vassals of Burgundy at
Troyes, and asked them whether they wanted him, now that
Warnhar was dead, to elevate another person to the same degree
of honor. But they were all unanimously opposed to electing a
Mayor of the Palace, and, working persistently on the king's
good will, they got him to agree." Under this head we should
also consider disputes among princes that seemed to endanger
the commonwealth, since these were settled in this same council. . . . [Several examples follow, mostly dealing with inheritance disputes among princes of the blood.]

And now we may look at other powers, for I find that, if
a prince or other person of high birth was charged with any
crime, he was summoned to this council and there compelled
to make his case. . . . [Two examples follow.]

As to divisions of the royal patrimony and appanages, documentation exists in Aimon *(V, 94),* where, speaking of Charlemagne, he says: "After settling these matters, the emperor held assembly with the leading men and nobles to make and keep peace among his sons, and to divide the kingdom into three parts so that each of them should rule and defend his own portion, in case they should survive him." . . . [Two more examples follow.]

From other passages, moreover, we may note that when a king planned to make major expenditures, such as building churches or founding monasteries, he asked the advice of the Estates. Thus Aimon *(IV, 41),* where he is speaking about Clovis II, who was seated on his throne before the solemn council: "This," says Aimon, "was the preface to his speech: 'Fellow Franks, . . . the duties of our earthly rule require us to call you together to consult on public matters.'"

So much then for these examples. We believe they very clearly prove what I said at the beginning, that the whole power of administering the kingdom was clearly vested in the public council, which, as we said above, was called the *"placitum."* This is because the term *placitum* in Latin usage referred to something that had been investigated and debated by many men in consultation, and on which they finally agreed, whence the expression *placita* of the philosophers in Cicero and other ancients. And since this is so, there is no absurdity, I think, in the conjecture, which I have expounded in other books of mine, that the common formula, *"Quia tale est nostrum placitum"* ("Because such is our *placitum*"), which royal clerks still use at the conclusion of laws and ordinances, derives from that word *placitum.* All of these used to be written in Latin, as is clear enough, we think, from Aimon's *Capitulary of Charlemagne* and other records of that sort. But later on, when the royal clerks began to use the vernacular, they unwittingly, or perhaps craftily, translated the phrase as *"Car tel est nostre plaisir"* ("Because such is our pleasure").*

And the power of the people is also indicated by the passage in Charlemagne's *Capitulary:* that the people should be ques-

Placitum is a noun made from the past participle of the verb *placere,* meaning to please or to be agreeable.

tioned concerning the chapters newly added to the law, and after all had consented, they were to put their signatures and confirmations on these chapters. From this it is clear that the people of France used to be bound of old only by those laws which they had sanctioned by their votes in the assembly. And so also at the end of *Lex Alemannorum:* "This is decreed in the presence of the king, his princes, and the entire Christian population within the kingdom of the Merovingians." Likewise, Aimon *(V, 38):* "In this *placitum* these terms were agreed upon between them with the consent of their followers. The agreement that was made between these glorious kings, both through their own consent and with the approval and consent of their followers [etc.]"

We should mention, finally, that the reputation of this council was so high among foreign peoples that even foreign princes, if they had some controversy, might sometimes submit it for judgment by that council. . . .

Chapters XII–XIV

[Chapter XII describes the office of Mayor of the Palace under the Merovingians. Power gradually accumulated in the mayors' hands to the point where Pippin, the last mayor of the palace, was able to seize the kingship. Hotman is willing to concede that the later Merovingians were often inert and incompetent, but he warns that their vices have apparently been exaggerated by historians like Einhard who were employed by the Carolingians to justify their dynasty. Certain more recent writers are reproved for having followed Einhard uncritically.

Chapter XIII criticizes the historical tradition according to which Pippin was created king by Pope Zacharias. Then, as always, Hotman argues, the crown was conferred by the people, and although the Pope did indeed participate, his role was merely advisory, not resolutive. "Although the Franks consulted the Pope before they made Pippin king, this does not mean that he was created by the Pope's command and authority. It is one thing to create a king, another to give advice about creating one; the right of creating is one thing, the right of advising is another; and in matters of this sort no one even has a right of giving counsel unless he has been asked."

Chapter XIV discusses the origins of the office of Constable, which replaced that of Mayor of the Palace, and also the origins of the twelve Peers of France. Hotman argues that the Peers do not go back to the beginnings of the kingdom but are a later institution with many feudal characteristics. For lack of better evidence Hotman is willing, at least provisionally, to accept an account that attributes their introduction to King Arthur of England, who at one time ruled part of France. But he is careful to point out that there is no clear evidence of their existence prior to the time of Philip the Fair. In later editions of the *Francogallia,* he adds that the Peers were a Capetian institution, originating with or consolidated by Hugh Capet. The honor of witnessing royal coronations was given to certain great nobles in order to enhance the ceremonial. In addition, a court of peers was constituted to hear serious charges against very high personages when the judicial functions of the public council were transferred to the Parlement of Paris.]

Chapter XV

On the continuing authority of the sacrosanct council under the Carolingian kings

The form of our commonwealth and the authority of the public council under the Merovingian kings have, we think, been sufficiently explained, so that we may now go on to describe their character in Carolingian times. And as far as we can judge from studying all of the historians, both French and German, the authority of the Orders, or Estates, remained unchanged, and sovereign judgment and decision of all questions lay, not in Pippin, or Charles, or Louis, but in the royal majesty itself, the true and proper seat of which was the solemn council, as we have shown above. . . . [Documentation is provided from Einhard and Aimon.]

This and all of the preceding passages are narratives about King Charles, to whom all nations gave the surname "the Great" for the greatness of his deeds in extending his kingdom over almost all of Europe. Yet Charles was unable to deprive the Franks of their original right and liberty, nor did he even try to embark on any major project without a decision by the people and authorization by the nobles. And after Charlemagne departed from this life, it is clear enough that his son Louis administered the kingdom on the same condition. . . . [Documentation is provided from Aimon.]

But to go on with particular examples would be endless and, I think, superfluous. For I believe that the instances already cited make it evident to all that up to Charles the Simple, that is, for more than 550 years, the sovereign judgment and decision of all affairs of state remained in the assembly of the people, or as we now call it, the Assembly of the Estates. And this institution of our forefathers has been held so sacred for so many centuries that I hardly know what to make of certain recent authors who shamelessly assert that initiation of the public council should be attributed to King Pippin, and this despite the fact that Einhard, the chancellor of Charlemagne, distinctly attests that it was a regular practice, under all the Merovingians, to hold a public assembly of their people every year on the first of May, and that they were brought to that assembly in a wagon drawn by oxen.

But to argue now from general principles, and to contemplate the wisdom of our forefathers as it is mirrored in this institution, is it not abundantly clear that they were well aware of the difference between a kingdom and a king? For the fact of the matter is that the king is the chief, particular and single; whereas the kingdom is the entirety of citizens and subjects, which is a distinction also noted by the jurists. Thus Ulpian defines a traitor as someone "who has hostile intent towards the commonwealth or the prince." And similarly in the *Lex*

Saxonica (title 3): "Anyone who conspires against the kingdom or the king of the Franks will be punished by death." Furthermore, the relationship of king to kingdom is the same as that of father to family, of guardian to orphan, of custodian to minor, of captain to ship at sea, and of general to army. Therefore, as the ward is not created for the sake of the guardian, nor the ship for the captain, nor the army for the general, but the latter for the former, so a people is not sought and procured for the sake of the king, but a king for the people. For a people can exist without a king, by following its own counsel or that of its nobles, whereas a king without a people cannot even be imagined.

Now let us look at other differences. A king is mortal, like any private person; the kingdom is perpetual and, at least in principle, immortal, as are guilds and corporations, according to the jurists. A king's mind may become troubled or affected with insanity, as with our Charles VI, who gave his kingdom to the English, nor are there any men whose mental balance is more easily disturbed by voluptuary pleasures. But a kingdom has its own unfailing source of wisdom in its elders and experienced statesmen, who are, so to speak, its mind. A king may be beaten in a single battle, in a single day, and may be captured and taken off to foreign territory, which, as none are unaware, is what happened to St. Louis, to Jean [II], and to Francis I. But when a king is lost, the kingdom still remains intact and, when the misfortune is reported, a council is convened, the chief men meet, and they seek a remedy for present dangers, which is what was done in the cases we have mentioned. A king, from infirmity of age or levity of character, may not only be seduced and depraved by some greedy, rapacious, and lustful counsellor or other, or by a group of licentious young companions, but he may even become so infatuated with a young girl as to give her almost the entire power of running the kingdom; and few, I think, are unaware how often examples of this evil have occurred. But a kingdom is continually supported by the advice and wisdom of its elders. Even Solomon, the wisest man of all, was corrupted by young girls, even in his very old age; Rehoboam, by young men; Ninus, by his mother, Semiramus; Ptolemy Auletes, by musicians and singers. Our forefathers allowed our kings to choose private counsellors of their own to look after all their private business. But the choice of senators, who were to administer the commonwealth, who were to consult together and guide the king in administering the kingdom, was reserved for the public assembly. In 1356, when King Jean was captured by the English and taken to England, a public council of the kingdom was held at Paris, and when some of the king's counsellors appeared there, they were ordered to leave the assembly and were told that the deputies to the public council would no longer meet unless the counsellors stayed away from that temple of the kingdom. And the evidence for this is to be found in the *Grandes Chroniques, II,* under King Jean, fol. 169.

And there never was an age that failed to recognize this clear distinction between the kingdom and the king. The king of the Spartans and the ephors, Xenophon attests, took an oath to each other every month. The king swore to rule according to the law, the ephors, to preserve the royal government if the king performed his promise. Cicero, in a letter to Brutus, *(II, V, 1)* says: "You know that I have always wanted our commonwealth to be free, not only of a king, but of kingship *(regno)*." Similarly, in his *De legibus (III, VII, 15):* "But since the royal form of commonwealth was once accepted and was repudiated later for the faults of a king and not of kingship, it will seem that only the title "king" was rejected, etc."*

---

*In subsequent editions, Hotman also cites the difference between the tenure of the king's personal servants and that of royal officers, or officers of the crown. When a king dies, the former are dismissed, because they depend directly on his person. The latter continue in office, because they were originally appointed by the public council and are not subject to removal at the king's discretion.

Chapter XVI

On the Capetian family, and the transfer to it of the kingdom of Francogallia

It has been shown above that over a period of 1,200 years the kingdom of Francogallia has been held by only three families, of which the first was the Merovingian and the second the Carolingian—so called from the names of their respective founders and heads. For even though succession was conferred, as we have often said, not by heredity, but by decision of the council, the Franks willingly retained the practice of their fellow Germans who, as Tacitus says, "chose their kings for nobility and their generals for valor." And so they most often chose their kings from those who were born of royal blood and were trained and educated in a royal manner, either as children or as relatives. But in 987, on the death of Louis V, the thirty-first king of France and the twelfth Carolingian, there was a transfer of the sceptre and an alteration of the royal line. There was, in fact, a surviving member of that family in Charles, the Duke of Lorraine, the deceased king's paternal uncle, to whom it seemed the succession should be given according to established practice. But Hugh Capet, the son of the Emperor Otto I's sister Havuide and a man of outstanding military reputation, came forward and demanded preference, because, as he put it, he was there whereas Charles was absent, and because he deserved well of the kingdom, while Charles had acted like a foreigner. For, during certain controversies between the German Empire and the kingdom of France, Charles had shown that he was on the side of partisans of the Empire and of strangers to the French kingdom, for which reason he had alienated the hearts and minds of a great many Frenchmen. . . . [An account of warfare between Charles and Hugh Capet follows. Among other things, it is indicated that Capet's main source of strength was the favor of the French nobility.]

And we should not fail to mention Capet's clever strategy in consolidating his new kingdom. In olden times the magistracies and high dignities of the kingdom, which are known as "duchies" and "counties," were conferred in the assembly of the people on men who were elected and appointed, and who held the office only as a benefice and, as the jurists say, on precarious tenure (as was shown in explaining the authority of the public council). But to win and hold the favor of the nobles, Hugh Capet made these honors, which until then had been temporary, permanent, and ordained that those who held them could retain them as patrimonial possessions and convey them to their children and posterity along with the rest of their legacy, my authority for which is the jurist, Francis Connan, *Commentarii, II, 9.* This manoeuvre of Capet's was no slight diminution of the public council's authority, although, considering the nature of the times, it does not seem likely that he could have done this all alone without the consent of the council itself.

Chapter XVII

On the continuing authority of the public council under the Capetian kings

As we may learn from Froissart, Monstrelet, Gaguin, Commines, Gilles, and all the other historians [of this period], the authority of the public council was hardly less under the Capetian dynasty than under the two preceding. But since it would be wearisome and endless to go through all the cases, we will select a few of the more famous ones to serve as a sample of the rest. . . . [Seven citations follow, one dealing with succession to the throne; another, with the adjudication of a dispute between two dukes; four, with regency arrangements; and one, with a decree of the Parlement of Paris voiding certain domain alienations of Francis I on the grounds that they had not been authorized by the Estates General.]

Chapter XVIII

On the memorable authority of the Council against King Louis XI

The great and inviolable strength and power of the Council and assembled Estates is evident from the preceding examples. But since we are engaged in this discussion, we should not leave out an occasion, within our fathers' memory, when the council's authority was invoked against King Louis XI, who is considered to have been the most cunning and devious of our kings. Around 1460, as a result of Louis' misgovernment of the kingdom and his frequent neglect of the duties of a good and patriotic prince, people began to clamor for a council, which would, by its authority, hold a general inquiry into the condition of the commonwealth. And since it was thought that the king would almost surely not submit to one, the magnates of the kingdom, aroused by the repeated complaints and demands of the commoners, began to gather their forces and assemble an army so that they would be able to advance the public welfare and, in the words of Philip Commines *(Memoires, I, 2)*, "forcibly confront the king with the ruined condition of the commonwealth's administration. They wanted to be prepared and ready with an army, so that if the king evaded consultation on the public welfare and refused to follow good advice, they could compel him to do so by force of arms, for which reason that war was said to have been undertaken for the public good and is commonly called the 'War of the Public Good.' "

The names of these notables are recorded by Commines, Gilles, and La Marche as follows: The Duke of Bourbon; the Duke of Berry, the king's brother; the Counts of Dunois, Nevers, Armagnac, and Albret; and the Duke of Charolois, who held supreme command. Wherever they marched, they proclaimed that they had begun the war for the public good and announced immunity from tributes and taxes (which is all from Gilles, *IV,* fol. 152), and they sent ambassadors to Paris with letters to the Parlement, clergy, and rector of the University (all of this again from Gilles, on the same folio), so that they would not think that the army had been raised to harm the king and would call upon the king to do his duty as the public need demanded.

Furthermore, the text of the annals that are entitled *Chronicles of Louis XI,* and which were printed at Paris by Galliot du Près, is essentially as follows (fol. 27): "The first and most important point in their demands was that an assembly of the Three Estates should be convened, since it alone, throughout the centuries, had been the remedy for every evil and had always had the power of healing misfortunes of this sort."* Again (fol. 28): "The magnates' ambassadors were heard at Paris on the 24th at the Town Hall in a meeting attended by deputies from the University, the Parlement, and the magistrates. Reply was made that their demand seemed thoroughly fair, and a council of the Three Estates was announced." These, I say, are the very words of the historian (fol. 28), and they attest the great truth of that old saying of Mark Antony: "Although all rebellions are always troublesome, there are some that are just, and even necessary." But the most just and most necessary of all is when a people oppressed by a savage tyrant begs assistance from a lawful assembly of citizens. And so Gaguin in his life of this same Louis uses these words where he describes the response of Charles, Duke of Burgundy, to the king's ambassadors: "Charles heard the ambassadors," he says (page 265), "and replied that there was nothing more likely to bring peace than an assembly of the Three Estates, for that is where discords and hostilities as deep as these are properly resolved. And after the ambassadors reported this by messengers to the king, Louis, now resting his hopes on delay, announced a council at Tours for the 1st of April, 146[8]. At the time set for the meeting, there were present from the entire kingdom, etc."

*Giesey notes that this refers to Jean de Roye's *Chronique Scandaleuse* and distorts the passage. According to de Roye, what was demanded was an assembly of the princes of the blood, not a meeting of the Three Estates. The mistake, however, all the more clearly shows how much Hotman wished to point the history of Louis XI to the needs of his own time.

The same is reported in so many words in the *Chronicles* that have been mentioned (fol. 64), and in the *Grandes Chroniques* (Vol. IV, fol. 242), where the following is added—which should be remembered and noted very carefully: that it was decided in this council that tested and proven men should be elected from the several orders to reform the commonwealth and (I am quoting word for word) to establish law and justice. And so also N. Gilles in the passage we have mentioned: "After the battle of Montlerinum," he says, "several judicious and prudent men were elected guardians of the public good as the king and the aforementioned great nobles had agreed; and first among these guardians was the Count of Dunois, who had initiated the rebellion." As we have said above, the old custom, after the wealth of the clergy had grown so enormous, was to divide the people into three orders, with the clergy occupying one of them, and so when these guardians were established, twelve were elected from each order. Thus, it was decided in this council that thirty-six guardians should be appointed who in joint consultation would remedy the public's ills. Monstrelet (Vol. IV, fol. 150) writes: "It was decreed, first, that, to reform the commonwealth and to remove the burden of taxes and other hardships from the common people, thirty-six men should be created by royal authority—twelve from the clergy, as many from the nobles, and an equal number from those learned in law and justice—who should be given the power to see what vices and evils the kingdom labored under and to remedy these vices. And the king gave his royal word and promise (or, verbatim, the king promised on the king's word) that he would ratify anything these thirty-six men decreed." Thus Monstrelet, whom Olivier La Marche in Chapter 35 of his History confirms almost word for word, reports the same number of thirty-six guardians of the commonwealth. At the same time La Marche also describes the frightful war, lasting almost thirteen years, that flared up in Francogallia when the king did not stand by his word and promise and broke the public faith he had publicly sworn. The king's perjury was expiated by his own infamy and the people's ruin.

But however this may be, it is very clear that less than a

hundred years have passed since the liberty of Francogallia, and the solemn authority of the council, showed vigorous life against a king who was neither young in age nor weak of mind, but who was already over forty and was endowed with more ingenuity than any of our other kings. Hence it is easy to see that our commonwealth, founded and established in liberty, has held fast to that free and inviolable condition for more than 1,500 years and even defended it by force and arms against the might of tyrants.

And we should not omit the noble comment on this subject by that distinguished man and most elegant historian, Philip Commines, who in his *Memoires (V, 19),* expressed the following opinion, which we shall render word for word: "Therefore, to proceed with the discourse I began, is there a king or prince in all the world who has the right to levy one penny of tribute on his subjects without their consent and against their will, unless he wishes to practice tyranny and violence? But, someone may reply, 'a time may come when one should not wait for a council of the people, when affairs do not permit such long delay.' But in going to war there is no need for so much haste; there is enough time to make abundant preparations for it. And I would add that kings and princes are more powerful and more formidable to their enemies when they go into war with the consent of their countrymen." And similarly, a little further on. "The king of France should be the last to use such phrases as 'I have the power to take from my subjects as I please.' For neither he nor any other prince has that kind of power. Those who speak like this do themselves no honor by it and do not increase their authority and reputation among foreign peoples. On the contrary, they inspire terror in their neighbors, who would not have such a person as their ruler under any circumstances. But if our king, or those who praise his power, were to say, 'I have such gentle and obedient subjects that they do not refuse anything I ask, and no other prince has subjects who are that obedient and who are more willing to forget their misfortunes and calamities,' it would be his glory and his ornament. For the following does not become a king: 'I take as I please; I have the power, and I mean to keep it.'

King Charles V never talked this way. And I have never heard any king of ours use words like that, but only certain of their courtiers and ministers, who seem to be doing them a service. But in my judgment they were injuring their masters and only spoke the way they did to flatter, without sufficiently considering what they said. And to offer even clearer proof of the gentle temper of the French, let us consider the council of the Three Estates that met at Tours in 1484, after the death of our King Louis XI. There was some opinion at that time that this good assembly of the estates was dangerous; and there were some, I know not who, but men of little worth, who said then, and have often said since, that it is high treason to speak of calling an assembly of the Three Estates. The truth, however, is that it is they who are committing that crime against God, and the king, and the commonwealth. Words of that sort are of no use to anyone but those who obtain honors and offices without merit of their own; who are unsuited to the offices they occupy; who have learned only how to flatter, and to please the ears, and to prattle about trifles; and who dread large assemblies of men, for fear that they will be recognized for what they are, and that their works will be denounced."

Chapter XIX

[Chapter XIX raises the question whether women are debarred not only from inheriting the crown, but also from becoming regents. Hotman concedes that the kingdom had in fact been administered by women on some occasions, especially by widowed queen-mothers. But he argues that reason rules these cases out as precedents, since someone who cannot be ruler in her own right cannot be eligible to govern for another. In any case, the public council has the right to make what it regards to be the best arrangement for a regency.

Most of the chapter is devoted to describing the tragic evils that follow from the rule of women, as indicated by a number of examples from French history in which a woman either obtained the position of regent or ruled informally through influence over her husband or children. Most of this is obviously directed against Catherine de Medici who is not, however, mentioned, since the illustrations are taken only from the past.]

Chapter XX

On the judicial Parlements

Under the Capetian dynasty a judicial kingdom sprang up in Francogallia, of which we ought to speak in view of the incredible industry of its builders and their unheard of ingenuity throughout the ages. Everywhere in France today a class of men predominates whom some call lawyers; others, pleaders. So great was the cunning of these men about 300 years ago that not only have they now almost completely overthrown the authority of the public council, which we have spoken of above, but they have forced even the princes of the kingdom, and royal majesty itself, to do obeisance to their grandeur. And so in every town where a seat of this kingdom is located, nearly a third of the citizens and residents, attracted by the great rewards, have applied themselves to the practice and study of the art of verbal brawling, as may be observed by anyone at Paris, which is ranked as first among these towns. For could anyone stay even for three days in that city without observing that a third of the citizens are deeply involved in the practice of that brawling and litigious art? The supreme assembly of pleaders there, which is called the purple-robed Senate, is so wealthy and so honored that, as Jugurtha once said of the Roman Senate, it seems not to be a group of councillors, but a gathering of kings and satraps, since anyone coopted into it, however low his birth, amasses all but royal riches in a few years' time. Many other cities, therefore, strain every nerve to become seats for judicial bodies of this sort, so that we may now count seven of these celebrated Parlements: the Parlements of Paris, Toulouse, Rouen, Grenoble, Bordeaux, Aix, and Dijon, all of which are fixed and stationary. An eighth, which is called the "Great Council," is moveable and itinerant. Within the borders of these kingdoms, furthermore, there are lower courts, or satrapies, as one might call them, which imitate the grandeur of the higher so far as they are able and are commonly known as "presidial courts." So great, then, is the virulence and contagion of this plague that, just as a good part of the Egyptians were occupied in building pyramids and other massive structures of that sort at the command of their tyrants, most of the French nation consumes all its energies in prosecuting law-suits and chicaneries, and in writing legal briefs.

The term "parlement" *(parlamentum),* in the ancient language of our people meant a conference of many men coming together from various places to deliberate on common concerns. Hence whenever princes or the emissaries of princes met to negotiate on peace or war, our old chronicles call the joint conference a "parlement." And for the same reason, in our ancient tongue the public council of the estates was called a "parlement."

But since the authority of this council was so great, and the Capetians were working to reduce it, they substituted a number of reliable senators for the council, transferred the august name "parlement" to that senate, and assigned it the following authority: First, no royal law or ordinance would be valid unless these councillors had approved and authorized it; second, every magistrate anywhere in France, including not only civil but even military officers, would be inaugurated through its approval and required to take their oaths to uphold the law before it; and finally, all of the power, dominion, and authority, which, as we have shown, was vested in the public council for so many years, was usurped in its entirety by that counterfeit Senate, into which the kings made sure that no one was coopted who they did not think would be useful for their plans. . . .

[A learned discussion of the history of the Parlements now follows, which is designed to show that they are of relatively recent origin and go back no further than the early fourteenth century or thereabouts. Before this time there were no sedentary courts, and law-suits were few and simple. In an older and better day St. Louis had administered justice personally, sitting under an oak tree and appealing to simple principles of law and equity. The subsequent complication of procedures is traced to the introduction of Roman legal styles via the papal court at Avignon. This complexity of law and procedure and a general spirit of litigiousness are now promoted by the Parlement.*]

Appendix [Francogallia, *Third Edition, Chapter XXV, 1586*]

The king of France does not have unlimited dominion in his kingdom but is circumscribed by settled and specific law

It has been sufficiently demonstrated, we believe, that the kings of France have not been granted unmeasured and unlimited power by their countrymen and cannot be considered absolute. It has been shown, rather, that they are bound by definite laws and compacts, the first and most important of which is that they must hold the authority of the public council sacred and inviolate and call it into solemn session in their presence as often as the public interest demands. But since the laws to which the king is bound are very numerous, we shall expound only those which none will question unless he has lost his reason or has become an enemy to his country, parents, and children.

*In subsequent editions, Hotman also links the expansion of the Parlements to the sale of offices by avaricious kings, and the corrupting effects of venality on the quality of justice are attacked at length. The appearance of a specialized Canon Law is added to the list of causes accounting for French litigiousness. The basic remedy is to rely on the Bible alone.

The first, then, is that nothing which affects the interest of the public as a whole may be decided by the king without the authorization of the public council. The imprint of this rule, the ancient force of which has been thoroughly documented, remains clear and explicit to this very day, in that the Senate at Paris, which appropriated a large part of the ancient parliament's authority, permits no edict to be ratified which has not been investigated by it and approved by the judgments of its councillors. It may well be said, then, that the authority of this Senate is similar, in this respect, to the power of the tribunes of the people who, as Valerius Maximus writes, used to wait outside the Senate House until the decrees of that order were brought out to them. They then examined these decrees in council, and if they seemed advantageous to the common people, the tribunes endorsed them with the letter "T" as an indication and sign of their assent. But if not, they exercised their right of veto and of intercession. We should note, however, that the learned Budé finds a different parallel. "As the Senate," says Budé, "was supposed to authorize all decisions of the people, for which we now use the Greek term *homologare,* so the ordinances of our princes are without force or sanction today unless enactments of this sort which concern the commonwealth have been authorized and promulgated by the Parlement *(Curiam).*" And a little later on he says: "It is in this court that provincial officers and judges, called *"baillis," "seneschaux,"* etc., generally swear allegiance to the law. It is in the record of this court's acts that charters and royal grants are registered to make them permanent and inextinguishable. It is by this court's authority that the acts of princes are ratified or repudiated in order to forestall refusals to enforce them. This is the one court, indeed, from which "absolute" princes are willing to receive law and yet maintain a civil temper, for they need its authorization to get their orders ratified and promulgated. They may want their ordonnances to escape the censure of this body, and their edicts to pass untouched; but they also want to have their enactments confirmed for all eternity by its decrees." Therefore, either the Senate has tyrannically usurped this power to veto royal edicts and commands, which is surely not believ-

able, or else our kings were never permitted absolute and un-
limited power to begin with, which is what Auffrerius, Bohier,
Montaigne, Chasseneux, and other jurists of great repute in
France attest with perfect unanimity.

Now, then, for the other fundamental laws *(leges regias)*
and, to begin with, the rule that the king is not entitled to
adopt a son or to dispose of his kingdom either *inter vivos* or
by testament, but that the institutions of our forebears and our
ancient customs have to be observed. "Now, as in the past,"
writes Jean Terre Rouge *(Tractatus, I, conc. 9)* "the kings of
France cannot transmit the kingdom as a legacy, nor make
their first-born or any other heir its ruler. And although succession obtains in France by force of custom, it is not the tacit
will of an intestate king that confers successors any more than
succession is or can be conferred by the explicit and testa-
mentary disposition of the king. It is custom, and custom only,
that confers the kingdom on a successor." . . .

[The nullification of the treaty between Charles VI and
Henry IV is cited as an illustration. Charles had promised to
adopt Henry as his son and successor. The French subsequently
argued that Charles had no power to alter the French law of
succession by which his natural son was designated next in
line.]

We shall call the above the second fundamental law of the
French kingdom, and now take up the third, which is as follows. When a king dies, the inheritance of the kingdom passes
to his oldest son, and the king is not permitted to substitute a
younger for the older son nor to designate any other successor
on his own authority. The reason for this rule is evident. Parents
are entitled to deprive their children of benefits proceeding from
themselves as parents, but they do not have this right where
the benefits are conferred by natural or customary law. *(Digest,
I, 7, 22; XLVIII, 22, 31.)* The oldest son obtains his birth-
right *(suitatem)* and expectation of inheritance not through the
favor of his parents but as a privilege of common law; he
properly receives this status not from his father but from the law
and institutions of our ancestors. Thus, all the doctors of civil
law are agreed that the king of the French cannot deprive his

first-born son of the rights of primogeniture [nor] confer the expectation of succession either on the second-born or anybody else. . . .

[A number of authorities are cited, with long quotations from Jean Terre Rouge and Guillaume Benedictus especially. It is pointed out, in the course of this, that technically the French king cannot will the kingdom even to his first-born son, since the status of the latter derives exclusively from custom.]

We now come to the fourth fundamental law, already discussed in Chapter X [1st Ed., Ch. VIII], by which no female may inherit the kingdom, so that the closest agnate male relative of the deceased king, no matter how remote, is preferred to any female relative. . . . This question was sharply posed after the death of Philip the Fair, who left one daughter, named Isabella, and three sons. Edward, King of England, married Isabella and had a son by her, who was also called Edward and who succeeded to the English throne at the time that Philip died. The three sons of Philip, who succeeded to the throne in turn, all died without male issue, so that Philip of Valois, the son of Philip's brother Charles, succeeded to the throne with the approval of the twelve Peers of France, who did not wish to give the kingdom either to Isabella, Queen of England, or to her son Edward. Hence, vast wars between the kings of France and England broke out, but unjustly, because just as the king's daughter does not succeed to the French crown, neither does her son. . . .

The fifth fundamental law relates to the royal domain and has also been discussed above. The king is not allowed to alienate any part of his domain without the authorization of the public council; for it was put at his disposal only to maintain his dignity as king, and the king's power over his domain is like that of a husband over his wife's dowry. Thus, when Charles VI transferred a portion of the domain to Count Sampaulinus in 1399, either as a gift or for some other reason, the Senate at Paris, substituting for the older Parliament or Estates, vetoed the grant and decreed that no alienation of domain is valid unless the Senate at Paris has authorized it. Papon has included this declaration in his *Arrests* (*V*, title 10), where many other Senate decrees *(Senatusconsulta)* of this sort are recorded. From all of these it is clearly settled law that alienation of domain by the king, without examination and approval by the Senate, is null and void. And when the Senate investigates, it most especially wants to know the following. Could the money not be taken from another source? Is the price suitable, and does it represent the last and highest bid at a regular public auction?

And on this it is worth quoting the opinion of Claude Seyssel, which we translate from his *Monarchie de France, I, 1:* "The third rein by which the kings of France are held in check is the legal order *(politia),* that is, the institutions and practices of the realm retained through many ages and confirmed by custom of long standing. The kings do not attempt to repeal these, and if they did, their enterprise would be in vain since their order would not be obeyed. The royal patrimony, or domain, furnishes a clear example. Kings have no right to alienate it except for great and necessary reasons, and these reasons have to be examined and approved by his council and by his Courts of Parlement and of Accounts. This examination is conducted so carefully and with such tenacity and so much discussion that very few people request alienations of this sort. Although our kings have the right to dispose of the fruits and revenues of the kingdom at their own discretion for as long as they hold the administration of the kingdom, the account of their expenditures, ordinary as well as extraordinary, is examined by the Chamber of Accounts. And if the king's expenditures seem to be unfounded, they are cut back. This fundamental law of the commonwealth is extremely helpful in preserving royal rule. For when the royal domain is exhausted, the usual remedy is to turn to taxes and extraordinary impositions, which are a burden on the common people. Thus, I need hardly say that this most excellent of fundamental laws restrains that excessive liberality of princes which tends toward prodigality."

And in II, 11, Seyssel adds: "A king, I repeat, can do nothing more agreeable to God or more to advance the interest of his fellow citizens and his own repute and dignity than to observe the fundamental laws of the realm. For he then acquires the name of good and Christian king and father of his country, as well as all the other names a great and glorious prince can acquire. But as soon as he goes beyond the bounds and limits prescribed to him and begins to substitute his own will for reason, he is considered bad, tyrannical, cruel, and intolerable, and he incurs the odium of God and of his countrymen." This, then, is the opinion of Claude Seyssel, who was Archbishop of Turin and Privy Councillor to Louis XII. . . . For the related opinion that kings of France may not alienate cities of the kingdom, see Hostiensis and Joannes Andreae on [*Corpus Juris Canonicum*] *XIII, X, 1, 33,* and Martinus Laudensis, in *Tractatus de confoederatione,* question 13.

As the sixth fundamental law we may take the rule, as stated by Bohier, that the king has no right to pardon crimes or remit capital punishment in the kingdom without the authorization of the Parlement. A convicted person bearing letters either of remission or of pardon, or exoneration, should be incarcerated and his letters laid before the Parlement, etc. (*Decisiones Burdigalenses,* 65)

The seventh is that the king may not remove any officer of the kingdom, or commonwealth, of France except for a cause recognized and proven in the Council of Peers, which is a law so well known and so often repeated throughout France that documentation is unnecessary.

And as the eighth fundamental law we may mention the rule that the king has no right to alter the coinage without authorization by the public council. Books 3 and 5 of Guillaume Budé's *De Asse* show, from all the ancient documents, that the right of coinage, the power, that is, of increasing or decreasing the value of money, was almost always in the people. Furthermore, Charles du Moulin, the most thorough student of monetary law, writes in the last commentary of his *De contractibus et usuriis* that he found a great many French laws in the archives of the *Parlement* and of the *Généraux des Monnaies* which declared that no alterations in the coinage could be made without the people's consent. In monetary changes, the consent of the people, whose interest is surely very great, was always part of the procedure. As the jurisconsults put it, in a matter of this sort, the consent of those who have an interest is necessary—or, to put it in another way, it must be approved by those it will affect. In addition, Hostiensis, the celebrated canonist, says in his treatise on assessments: "It is asked whether the king of France has the prerogative of granting tolls or of altering the coinage. I answer, as does the Pope in a similar question, that it has seemed so to some *(Corp. Jur. Can., c. 13, X, 4, 17).* But it does not seem so to me, unless the people have given him that power, as it was given to the emperor *(Dig. I, 2, 2, 6)."*

Part II

Right of Magistrates

Editor's Note

Theodore Beza, or de Bèze, (1519-1605) came from an affluent family of the lesser nobility. His early education and tastes were humanist. But in 1548, after a nearly fatal illness, he experienced a profound religious conversion and became a follower of Calvin. By the early 1560's he had become one of Calvin's closest associates as well as the leader of the Protestant churches in France. At the conference of Poissy, called by Catherine de Medici in 1561 to resolve the religious divisions between Catholics and Protestants, the French churches, with Calvin's consent, requested Beza to lead their delegation. In the first religious war of 1562-1563, Beza accompanied Condé and Coligny and wrote most of Condé's manifestoes. Beza continued to be active in Huguenot affairs and was the Moderator of the important synod of La Rochelle in 1571. But after 1564 his visits to France became exceptional. Upon the death of Calvin in that year, he was named to succeed Calvin as Moderator of the Company of Pastors at Geneva and thus became the leader of the Calvinist movement on the Continent. In 1580 Beza returned to the ranks as minister and teacher. In his later years his energies were undermined by chronic illness, and he retired completely in 1600, five years before he died.[1]

Most of Beza's writings after 1548 were devoted to religious themes. On the relationship of church and state and on ecclesiastical discipline, his position was very close to Calvin's. In his *De haereticis a civili magistratu puniendis* of 1554 he defended the execution of Servetus against an attack by Sebastian Castellio, who had argued for religious toleration. And he consistently opposed efforts by a part of the French Protestants, led by Jean Morely, to transfer control of discipline and doctrine from the pastors to the congregation.[2]

In the course of the *De haereticis* Beza already mentioned the possibility of resistance by inferior magistrates to defend the true religion.[3] Although he claimed to have had no part in the Conspiracy of Amboise,[4] which he thought was ill-advised, he apparently believed that resistance to the usurpation of the Guises was legitimate in principle. This, in any event, was the ground of his subsequent manifestoes for Condé. But as has already been indicated, these early thoughts were not elaborated until after the St. Bartholomew's Day Massacre. The broadening and deepening of his position in the *Right of Magistrates* probably owes much to the influence of Hotman whom Beza consulted at the time.[5]

The *Right of Magistrates* was disapproved for publication by the censors of the Geneva city council, presumably to avoid provocation of the French. It was published anonymously, probably at Heidelberg,[6] early in 1574, in the guise of a revised and expanded edition of the *Admonition* of Magdeburg.[7] Beza's authorship, however, is well established by the records of the Geneva council, to whom Beza had initially submitted it. These records also lead us to believe that the work was originally written in Latin—since it is referred to as *De jure magistratum*—and was later translated by Beza into French, which is the language of the first edition.[8] The first Latin edition of 1576 is advertised as a translation from the French.[9] But it may have been a version of the original Latin manuscript, and even if a retranslation from the French, it was probably by Beza's own hand.

The present translation is based upon the French edition, as it is reprinted in Simon Goulart, *L'éstat de France souvs Charles Neufiesme,* Meidelbourg, 1578, Vol. II. But it has been carefully checked against the critical Latin edition, based on the text of 1580, done by Klaus Sturm in 1965. The Latin version (or retranslation) follows the French very closely and faithfully. On the few occasions where minor discrepancies appear, the French variation is preferred since this was the language of the first and most influential edition. On the other hand, the subdivisions of the work are more clearly indicated in the Sturm edition, and the titles of the questions have been translated from the Latin.

A complete, if very literal, translation, based on the Latin edition of 1595, has been available since 1956.[10] The present translation is a rather full abridgment. A number of the examples, as well as the analogies and answers to objections, have been summarized or briefly indicated, whereas the citations of authorities in the margin have been mostly suppressed. The general argument, however, and the more important illustrations have been represented fully.

DV DROIT
DES MAGISTRATS
SVR LEVRS SVBIETS.

Traitté tref-neceſſaire en ce temps,
pour aduertir de leur deuoir, tant
les Magiſtrats que les Subiets: publié par ceux de Magdebourg l'an
M D L: & maintenant re-
ueu & augmenté de plu-
ſieurs raiſons & ex-
emples.

PSAL. 2.

Erudimini qui iudicatis terram.

1 5 7 4.

Right of Magistrates

I. Should magistrates as well as God be unconditionally obeyed?

The only will that is a perpetual and immutable criterion of justice is the will of the one God and none other. Hence Him alone we are obliged to obey without exception. Princes too would have to be obeyed implicitly if they were always the voice of God's commandments. But since the opposite too often happens, an exception is imposed upon obedience, when their commands are irreligious or iniquitous. Irreligious commands are those which order us to do what the First Table of God's Law forbids, or forbid us to do what it commands. Iniquitous commands are those that cannot be obeyed without violating or neglecting the charity we owe our fellow men according to our station public or private. And I can prove this assertion by evident reasons and examples. . . .

[Various passages and examples from Scripture are cited, the general tenor of which is that one must obey God rather than man.]

II. To what extent should a subject assume the justice of commands?

Having established this foundation, I shall be glad to examine in detail some related points that have troubled many consciences. First, it is often asked whether a magistrate is bound to justify all of his commands to everyone. I say no and hold rather that loyal subjects should presume well of their rulers and not inquire too closely into complicated matters that are beyond their grasp and station. But if their consciences are troubled nonetheless, they may and should inquire, by modest and pacific means, as to the reason and equity of what they are commanded to do or to refrain from doing. For the clear injunction of the Apostle still abides, that "anything done without faith (which is done, that is with a doubting conscience) is sin." (*Romans* 14:23) And, of course, if a command is clearly irreligious or iniquitous, what we have said above applies.

III. How far should disobedience extend?

It is also asked how far disobedience to irreligious or iniquitous commands of rulers should extend. My answer is that each man must have regard to his vocation, and whether it is general and public or is private.* If your magistrate commands you to do what God forbids, as did Pharaoh the midwives of Egypt and Herod when he ordered his followers to slay the innocents, it is your duty to refuse to act. . . . But if the tyrant forbids you to do what God has commanded, then you will not have done your duty merely by refusing to obey the tyrant, but you must render obedience to God. Thus, Obadiah not only refused to kill the prophets, but gave them refuge and nourishment against the will of Ahab and Jezebel. . . .

[The point is illustrated by further Biblical examples and is extended to all obligations under natural law.]

IV. What are the remedies of a subject injured by a lesser magistrate?

The further question now arises as to what a man of good conscience should do, not where he is asked to do a wrong, but where the wrong is done to him. This I hold to be a complicated question for which distinctions must be drawn.

If the magistrate who wrongs a subject is beneath another who is sovereign, the aggrieved subject may appeal to the sovereign according to the law, as St. Paul appealed to Caesar to prevent the wrong being done him by Festus, the governor of Judea. But here private subjects must keep two considerations in mind. They should proceed exclusively by legal means, and then only insofar as it is expedient. For when that same

---

*I.e., private subjects do not ordinarily receive commands to do what God forbids.

St. Paul was outraged and whipped at Philippi by an ill-advised magistrate acting contrary to his rights as a Roman citizen, and without even hearing his case, he decided that patience would better serve God's glory and pursued his rights no further, merely admonishing the magistrates for their violation of the law.

But if it should happen, as it does all too often in our time, that one of two lower magistrates does violence to the other, against the express will of their sovereign, then, I say, it is always licit for the aggrieved magistrate, after he has tried all milder means, to take his stand upon the law and to repel illegal violence by resort to arms, as Nehemiah did against Sanballat and his adherents.

V. Is resistance to a superior magistrate always illicit and seditious?

But what if the source of outrage should be the sovereign magistrate himself? Jesus Christ and all the martyrs afterwards surely teach us that injustice should be suffered patiently, and that it is the glory of Christians to suffer injustice at the hands of others while doing none themselves. Is there then no remedy at all, it will be asked, against a sovereign who abuses his dominion against all law divine and human? A remedy does exist, and it is to be found in human institutions, although in saying this I hope that no one will infer that I support those fanatic Anabaptists and other seditious and mutinous people who, I believe, deserve rather to be hated by all and to be punished severely for their crimes. For to put the matter properly, those who teach that notorious tyranny may be resisted in good conscience are not denying good and legitimate rulers the authority that God has given them, nor are they encouraging rebellion. On the contrary, the authority of magistrates cannot be stabilized, nor that public peace, which is the end of all true governance, preserved unless tyranny is prevented from arising or else abolished when it does. The question, then, is to see if there is some means, in accord with justice and the will of God, by which subjects may curb manifest tyranny on the part of a sovereign magistrate, by force of arms if need be.

To resolve this question I would begin by pointing out that peoples do not come from rulers; that peoples, whether they have chosen to be governed by a single prince or by a number of elected notables, are older than these rulers; and that peoples, accordingly, are not created for their rulers, but rulers rather for their peoples, just as a guardian is created for the ward, not the ward for the guardian, and the shepherd for the flock, not the flock for the shepherd. And although this is all self-evident, it can be confirmed by the history of every nation, for even God, having chosen Saul to rule in place of Samuel at the people's request, willed that the people, in addition, should establish and receive Saul as their king. David, too, though God's own choice, did not exercise royal power until he received the votes and free consent of the tribes of Israel. And although the right to the throne became hereditary in the line of David by divine decree (unless there was some exceptional obstacle, as when the Egyptians and then the kings of Assyria tyrannized God's people), it was arranged that of the race of David only he whom the people had approved should reign, so that although the kingdom was hereditary as to family because God had so ordained, it was nonetheless elective as to individuals. . . .

[There follow additional examples from the Old Testament, opinions of ancient philosophers, and citations to St. Paul.]

. . . [Y]et some people so recommend patience and prayers to God that they condemn all who do not yield their necks [to violence] as rebels and false Christians. So slippery is this terrain that I beg the reader to remember all that I have said above so as to draw no evil consequence from what I am about to say upon this point. I praise Christian patience as a virtue to be especially commended, and I avow that it is to be assiduously cultivated in men as the pathway to eternal bliss. I detest seditions and disorders of all kinds as horrible monstrosities, and I agree that in affliction most of all we should depend on God alone. I admit that prayers united with repentance are proper and necessary remedies to tyranny since it is most often an evil or scourge sent by God for the chastisement of nations. But for all of this, I deny that it is illicit for peoples oppressed by notorious tyranny to make use of lawful remedies in addition to repentance and prayers, and I now present the reasons for my view.

Rights of Subjects Against Usurpers

Assuming now what I have said above about the origin of kings and magistrates, it follows that those who, by force or fraud, have usurped a power that does not belong to them by law are not legitimate kings. And of such tyrants there are two varieties. There are those who usurp power against their fellow citizens contrary to established and accepted law, as did Caesar, who oppressed the Roman Republic under the assumed title of perpetual dictator, and other tyrants, mainly Greek, who suppressed their countries' liberty. Then there are others, not content with the territory in which their rule is lawful, who extend their boundaries at the expense of their neighbors' liberty; which is the way that empires have attained greatness ever since the world began. In witness of this we have the account of Nimrod in the Scripture, as well as frequent oppressions of the Israelites by neighboring peoples.

Of these tyrants, then, I say that since they had no rights over the people of God, the Israelites were not only bound to disobey their irreligious edicts, but could and should have resisted their unlawful violence, and that, accordingly, the heads of the tribes were much at fault for not uniting to defend their country from its enemies, assuming that they had the means. For it is a well-known rule of all law divine and human that even a private individual must use all his strength to defend his country from attack and especially when the question of religion is combined with that of liberty. And the pirate, who was captured and brought before Alexander the Great, surely spoke the truth when he dared to address Alexander in these terms: "What difference is there between you and me, except that you rob the world with a great navy and I with but a single ship?"

Nor is there any real objection in the assertion, relied upon by some, that it is God who transfers kingdoms and empires and who often gives the victory to tyrants. For may it please

God that I do not, on that account, agree with Lucan that God makes right of wrong, or that I condemn Demosthenes for defending his country's liberty against Philip of Macedon because Demosthenes lost and Philip won. And I use these [pagan] examples not as rules for Christian consciences, but because they are widely known and celebrated, and also because even the affairs of pagans are not so distant from the rule of equity that one cannot see that right is on the one side and wrong is on the other. I say then—as did Demosthenes when his opponent Aeschines reproached him on the unhappy outcome of the battle of Charoneia—that the justice or injustice of an enterprise should not be measured only by success. For, to put it in more Christian fashion, God often punishes the faults of men, or tests his faithful, by arranging that their plans, which may in themselves be good and just, should have a result very different from the one intended. A very clear example is the war of the other tribes of Israel against the tribe of Benjamin. Yet this is not to say either that God ever ceases to be just, no matter what instruments he uses, or that nations do not have a rightful case against oppressors even when their defeat is in accord with the just decree of God.

Hence, I cannot accept the opinion of those who, without exception or distinction, would condemn all slayers of tyrants, to whom, indeed, the Greeks of old gave honors and rewards. Nor do I share the view that finds the liberations mentioned in the Book of Judges to be so special and extraordinary that no general implications may be drawn from them. For even though the judges had an extraordinary divine inspiration for their acts, it does not follow that the magistrates of the Israelites and private persons also had no right under ordinary law to resist the tyranny of strangers whom the people had neither constituted nor accepted. And the fact that these deliverances were accomplished only by those whom God had specially employed in no way detracts from my contention, but only shows the torpor and faintheartedness of the Israelites, which was the just sentence of God for their iniquities.

Therefore, the correct inference from these examples, I believe, is that the middle path should be adopted. Where someone would seize dominion without title or has already usurped it—whether he comes from without or arises from within his country's womb, like a viper to kill her in his birth—the private citizen should appeal to the legitimate magistrates so that, if possible, the public enemy may be repulsed by public authority and by common consent. But if the magistrates, from connivance or whatever, should fail to do their duty, then each private citizen should exert all his strength to defend the legitimate institutions of his country (to which, after God, each man owes his whole existence) and to resist an individual whose authority is not legitimate because he would usurp, or has usurped, dominion in violation of the law.

But here it should be noted that defect [of title] at the beginning of a usurpation may subsequently be repaired. He who began as a tyrant may become a legitimate and inviolable magistrate through that free and lawful consent by which legitimate rulers are created. Thus, the war against Caesar by Pompey was just, even though Caesar was the winner. But if it is true that Caesar obtained sovereign dominion in the guise of a perpetual dictatorship through the free and willing consent of the Roman people, there could be no basis for debating whether the subsequent conspiracy against him was legitimate unless it could be shown that he had flagrantly abused that dictatorship. I also think it certain that good Roman citizens could and should have fought for the Republic against the Triumvirate. But I dare not say that Cinna and his followers could rightfully conspire to kill Augustus once the *lex regia,** as it is called, was promulgated and accepted.

Yet here too a distinction is required. It will be agreed, no doubt, that the consent of the whole people or its greater part, whether given freely or extorted through fear and violence, should not be kept, but broken, if it appears to be in manifest conflict with equity and honesty. For how can anyone believe that a people, knowingly and without constraint, would subject itself to someone in order to be destroyed and pillaged? But if it comes to rescinding or amending a promise of this sort, there are two main points to be observed: first, that it should

*See above, note on p. 12.

not be undertaken hastily, and second, that it should not be done riotously, as far as possible, but by orderly and peaceful means. . . .

[Two examples of invalid grants are cited, oaths of kings or peoples to the Papacy and the temporal jurisdiction of the Catholic Church.]

VI. Do subjects have any remedy against a legitimate sovereign who has become a notorious tyrant?

We must now take up a question which, not without reason, is hotly debated in our day. What in good conscience may be done by subjects if their sovereign magistrate, who is otherwise legitimate, becomes a notorious tyrant? Is the authority of a sovereign who has changed into a notorious tyrant so sacred and inviolable that subjects must endure him unresisting? And if they may resist, may they go so far as to resort to arms?

I reply that there are three kinds of subjects. Some are purely private persons who have no public office. Others, like the sovereign, are magistrates but are underneath him and so subaltern or inferior. The third class includes those who in ordinary matters do not exercise sovereign power but are established to check and bridle the sovereign magistrate. And as these classes differ, so must my answer vary.

Private Persons
As for private persons: if they have expressly and voluntarily consented to the dominion of a usurper, as the Roman people accepted Augustus and his successors, or if their legitimate ruler has become a notorious tyrant, as did Abimelech among the Israelites, the Thirty at Athens, the Decemvirs at Rome, and others elsewhere, then, I say, unless a private person has a special calling from God, which I do not deal with here, he may not, on his own initiative, answer force with force but must either go into exile or bear the yoke with trust in God (although, as was said at the beginning, he must never make himself the instrument of tyranny against another or fail to do his duty to God and to his fellow men).

Here our previous responses may perhaps be cited in objection. In discussing the two other kinds of tyranny, we said that even private persons were obliged to resist with all their strength. And at first glance it might seem that attempted usurpation by a private person and tyrannical use of legitimate dominion are the same, and that the same solution should apply in either case. But on closer inspection we discover a very considerable difference between these two cases, which appear to be so similar. A man who invades against others who are in no way subject to him (even if he wishes to rule equitably, as we read of Peisistratus and Demetrios of Phaleros at Athens) may rightfully be stopped by force of arms, and by anyone, no matter what his station, since there is no obligation whatsoever towards him. But a ruler who has been avowed by his people may abuse his dominion and still retain his authority over private subjects because the obligation to obey him was publicly contracted by common consent and cannot be withdrawn and nullified at the pleasure of a private individual. Were it otherwise, infinite troubles would ensue even worse than the tyranny itself, and a thousand tyrants would arise on the pretext of suppressing one.

And yet another argument, weightier than all the others that might be brought forward to the contrary, is the authority of God's word, which is unfailingly clear. St. Paul, speaking of the duty of a private citizen, not only forbids resistance to any magistrate, inferior as well as sovereign, but commands obedience for conscience's sake. St. Peter also orders us to honor kings, presumably remembering the reproof he received from his Master when, as a private person, he drew his sword against the public power, even though it was being misused against his Master. And yet there is none who does not know what kind of men the emperors of those days were, *i.e.,* Tiberius and Nero; or what most of the provincial governors were like. The same attitude was later adopted by the faithful martyrs who were cruelly persecuted by inhuman tyrants, and not only when emperors persecuted Christians according to imperial law, but even when they faithlessly transgressed standing edicts passed in favor of the Christians, as did the Emperor Julian the Apostate.

My conclusion, then, is that it is illicit for any private subject to use force against a tyrant whose dominion was freely ratified beforehand by the people. And if in private contracts a promise is so sacred that we must keep it even when it leads to loss, there is an even greater duty on the part of private persons not to disavow an obligation that was entered into by public agreement.

Lesser Magistrates

I come now to the lesser magistrates who hold a lower rank between the sovereign and the people. I do not mean officers of the king's household, who are devoted rather to the king than the kingdom, but those who have public or state responsibilities either in the administration of justice or in war. In a monarchy, therefore, the latter are called "officers of the crown," and thus of the kingdom rather than the king, which are two quite different things. Such, in [imperial] Rome, were the consuls, the praetors, the prefect of the city, the governors that were still appointed by the people and the Senate under the Empire, and similar officers of the Republic or of the Empire, who, for that reason, were called "magistrates of the Roman people" even in the period of the last emperors. In Israel they were the leaders of the twelve tribes; the captains of thousands, of hundreds, and of fifties; and the elders of the people. This arrangement, established under Moses, was not abolished with the change from aristocracy to monarchy, but was retained, and organized with more precision under Solomon. And in our day they are the officers of the various Christian kingdoms among whom may be numbered dukes, marquisses, counts, viscount, barons, and chatelains, whose estates and offices were at one time public and conferred in the ordinary legal way and have since become hereditary, without, however, any change in the nature of their right and their authority. And we must also include the elected officers of towns such as *maires, viguiers,* consuls, *capitouls,* syndics, *échevins,* and so on.

Now, although all these officers are beneath their sovereign in that they take commands from him and are installed in office and approved by him, they hold, properly speaking, not of the sovereign but of the sovereignty. That is why, when the sovereign magistrate dies, they nonetheless remain in office, just as the sovereignty itself remains intact. It is true that the newly succeeding administrator of the sovereignty confirms their dignities as also the privileges of towns (which is a custom first introduced into the Roman empire by the Emperor Tiberius according to Suetonius in his life of Vespasian, but which was unknown in ancient France, except in cases where the crown did not descend from father to son). But this does not imply that the sovereign is the author and source of their rights, since the sovereign himself does not enter into true possession of his sovereign administration until he has sworn fealty to the sovereignty and accepted the conditions attached to his oath, in the same way that he subsequently administers the oath to the above-mentioned officers. Hence confirmation of this sort resembles a feudal investiture where there is a new vassal or a new lord. It does not confer any new right but is simply the renewed recognition of an old one on the occasion of a change of persons.

It is thus apparent that there is a mutual obligation between the king and the officers of a kingdom; that the government of the kingdom is not in the hands of the king in its entirety, but only the sovereign degree; that each of the officers has a share in accord with his degree; and that there are definite conditions on either side. If these conditions are not observed by the inferior officers, it is the part of the sovereign to dismiss and punish them, but only for definite cause and according to the procedures prescribed by the law of the realm, and not otherwise, unless he is himself to violate the oath he took to exercise his office in conformity with law. If the king, hereditary or elective, clearly goes back on the conditions without which he would not have been recognized and acknowledged, can there be any doubt that the lesser magistrates of the kingdom, of the cities, and of the provinces, the administration of which they have received from the sovereignty itself, are free of their oath, at least to the extent that they are entitled to resist flagrant oppression of the realm which they swore to defend and protect according to their office and their particular jurisdiction?

What, it will be asked? Is a ruler, previously regarded as sovereign and inviolable, suddenly to be considered a private person at the whim of some subordinate, and then pursued and attacked as if a public enemy? Not at all, I say, for this would open the door to all kinds of miserable seditions and conspiracies. I am speaking, in the first place, of a clearly flagrant tyranny and of a tyrant who endures no remonstrations. Furthermore, I do not speak of removing a tyrant from his throne, but only of resistance against open violence according to one's rank, for I have already shown that an obligation entered into by common agreement cannot be nullified at the discretion of any individual, no matter who he is and no matter how just his complaint.

On the other hand, it is by the sovereignty itself that lesser officers are charged with enforcing and maintaining law among those committed to their charge, to which duty they are further bound by oath. (And they are not absolved from this oath by the delinquency of a king who has turned tyrant and flagrantly violated the conditions to which he swore and under which he was received as king.) Is it not then reasonable, by all law divine and human, that more should be permitted to these lesser magistrates, in view of their sworn duty to preserve the law, than to purely private persons without office? I say, therefore, that they are obliged, if reduced to that necessity, and by force of arms where that is possible, to offer resistance to flagrant tyranny, and to safeguard those within their care, until such time as the Estates, or whoever holds the legislative power of the kingdom or the empire, may by common deliberation make further and appropriate provision for the public welfare. This, moreover, is not to be seditious or disloyal towards one's sovereign, but to be loyal fully and to keep one's faith toward those from whom one's office was received against him who has broken his oath and oppressed the kingdom he ought to have protected.

This was the right on which Brutus and Lucretius acted against Tarquin the Proud at Rome (even though their private interests were involved to some extent as well). To resist flagrant tyranny, Brutus as tribune of the knights and Lucretius as prefect of the city assembled the Roman people, by whose authority the tyrant was driven from his kingdom and his possessions confiscated. And had they been able to lay hands on him, they would doubtless have condemned his person according to the law, which he had violated and not upheld as was his duty. For to say that the sovereign is not subject to the law is surely the false maxim of detestable flatterers, not of a subject loyal to his prince. On the contrary, there is not a single law to which the ruler is not bound in the conduct of his government, since he has sworn to be the protector and preserver of them all. . . .

[After quotations from Marcus Aurelius and Trajan, there follow two examples from Scripture: David's armed resistance against Saul for purposes of self-defense and the rebellion of the priestly city of Libnah against Jehoram.]

These two examples, quite apart from the arguments above, are, in my opinion, so clear and authentic as to give sufficient assurance to the consciences of lesser magistrates who, after trying every other remedy, find it necessary to resort to arms to protect those within their charge from flagrant tyranny, and thus seek not to stir up rebellion but to stop it. And it is well known that in the days of our forefathers the tyranny of those who ruled the Swiss was the occasion for the municipal magistrates of the Swiss to assert the liberty that people now enjoy.

The Estates and Similar Bodies

We must now speak of the third class of subjects, which, though admittedly subject to the sovereign in a certain respect, is, in another respect, and in cases of necessity, the protector of the rights of the sovereignty itself, and is established to hold the sovereign to his duty, and even, if need be, to constrain and punish him.

First, I would recall what I have said before, that the people is prior to all the magistrates, and does not exist for them, but they for it. It sometimes seems, of course, that certain peoples originated with the king. The Roman people, for example, seem to have been created by Romulus and were not, strictly speaking, an existing people but a multitude of persons culled from other peoples. Yet an exception of this sort is not the rule, and even Romulus had no dominion without that multitude's consent. Hence, the power of magistrates, however great or sovereign, derives from the power of the public that put them in their station, rather than the other way around. Nor may it be objected that although these magistrates had this status to begin with, the people later submitted themselves completely to the power and will of those they had accepted as their sovereigns and surrendered all their liberty freely and without reserve. For I deny that there is any evidence of such submission and hold, on the contrary, that wherever law and equity prevailed, nations neither created nor accepted kings except upon definite conditions. From this it follows that when kings flagrantly violate these terms, those who have the power to give *(baillir)* them their authority have no less power to deprive them of it. And it will now be shown that this was the practice of all of the most famous nations of all ages.

Let us begin with the Roman kingship and go on to the Empire, although these are not, of course, the oldest states. Livy, speaking of the earliest Roman kingship, expressly says that after the death of Romulus, who had fathered the people so to speak, the hundred *interreges* who then governed in rotation, were so disliked by the commoners that an agreement was made that henceforth kings should be created by vote of the people with confirmation by the Senate. The same author says of Tarquin the Proud, the last of the kings, "He had no claim to the throne but force, since he ruled neither by the decree of the people nor the authority of the Senate." And he then relates the acts of Tarquin that were contrary to ancient custom. "He was the first of the kings," says Livy, "to break with the custom handed down from his predecessors of consulting the Senate on all matters; and to run the commonwealth with private counsellors, making peace or war, alliances and confederations as he pleased, and with whomever he wished, without informing the people or the Senate." It is evident from this that the Roman kings were recognized only on definite conditions and that if these were not observed the people, assembled according to their civic ranks, had no less power to depose a king than to establish one, as was shown in the instance of that tyrant. Seneca, quoting Cicero's *Commonwealth,* remarks that appeal lay from the king to the people, as in the case of Horatius, who after killing his sister, was absolved by the people although he had been condemned by the judges of King Tullius Hostilius. And Dionysius further attests that when the Roman state was being formed by Romulus and his council, the king was made the guardian of the law, but the power of creating magistrates, making laws, and declaring war was left to the people. And this seems to have been the model for the founders of the French monarchy as will be shown below. . . .

[Further examples from early Roman history of the people's power over their rulers are given. There is brief comment on the constitutional position of the Decemvirs and the dictator. It is then argued that under the Empire some limitation of the ruler's power was still acknowledged as well as some right in the Senate to depose, although all of this was now obscured by frequent tyranny.]

Athens

As for the Athenians, when their democracy was overthrown and turned into an aristocracy, the histories of the time attest that the Athenians first established thirty men, and later ten, as governors, and that for abuse of their authority they were deposed and punished by the people, which thus exercised the same right by which it had created them.

Sparta

It is well known also that the Spartans freely selected their kings from the family of Hercules, an arrangement which, Plutarch tells us, Lysander sought in vain to change. Since the kings were elected with definite conditions, the Spartans established ephors to keep them in check. Some kings were exiled, others even suffered capital punishment. And the system lasted until the ephors were treacherously put to death by the tyrant Cleomenes, whereupon Sparta lost her empire together with her liberty. I am reminded here of the beautiful passage in Xeno-phon's *Commonwealth of the Lacedaemonians (XV, 7)*, where the king and the ephors are said to swear mutual obligation: ". . . the ephors in the name of all the citizens, the king in his own name; the king swearing that he will reign according to established law, the ephors that they will keep the city for him if he will keep his oath."

The Israelites

I now come to the government of the Israelites, incompar-ably the best that ever was, if only they had been content with it. What raised it up above the very skies was that at its begin-ning the Eternal Himself was its monarch, and not only in the sense that He is the sovereign Lord of all things, but in the more specific sense as well, in that He visibly gave the Law through Moses, then brought the people to the promised land through Joshua, and, finally, governed through the judges whom He alone had chosen. In this period, Israel's government was truly monarchy (although God made use of men as He saw fit). And if all kingdoms could be governed by this Monarch, or if kings would always be governed by Him who is sovereign of all the world, our present inquiry would be as superfluous as now it is necessary. But that happy government, which was given to no other people, was changed in a curious way. For whereas other monarchies change into tyrannies through the misdeed of the monarch, the Israelites, not appreciating their good fortune, constrained, so to speak, their true Monarch, who can never be a tyrant, to let them have a human king like other peoples. This was finally granted to them by the Lord, but granted in His wrath and anger, which was not because the monarchical state is of itself condemned by God, but because the people had insisted on a change. Nevertheless, it is a fact, which neither can nor ought to be disguised, that ever since the world began, there has never been a single monarch (even if we take the best) who has not abused his office. And philoso-phers, relying on natural reason, have also concluded that monarchical government is more often the ruin of a people than its preservation, unless the king is bridled so that the great good that can come from monarchy is yielded, and the enormous evil checked which it otherwise inevitably brings. I include these remarks as a preface to my discussion of Israel's government because the examples here are especially clear and evident. And it behooves both princes and peoples to mark them well so that neither of the two parties will be ruined by the other, but the Lord, on whom tranquility depends, will be glorified and those who rule as well as those who obey will be able to live comfortably.

But to return to my inquiry, the Lord, justly irritated by His people and wishing to teach them the consequence of their foolish impulse, foretold through Samuel what is referred to in that narrative as the right of kings and described in strange and remarkable terms. The essence of it is that the king would do as he pleased with the persons and goods of his subjects, which is the principle of tyranny, not of royal government. For it is beyond all reasonable doubt that only God's will is identical with reason, and that a thing need not be just as a condition of God's willing it, inasmuch as the very measure of justice is God's will. With men, on the contrary, reason itself must be regulated by good and holy laws—especially with men who govern others. Hence, they are much mistaken who take these words of Samuel as authorizing anything a king may please to do, as if to follow that execrable motto of a vile, incestuous woman: *"Si libet, licet,"* ("Right is anything I like"), which has been practiced all too often in our time. The words of Samuel must rather be understood as telling Israel: You are not content to have God as your monarch, as He has been up to now in a special and particular way, and you would have a king in the fashion of other peoples. You shall have your wish, but now behold what fine justice he will do you, and what equity he will show towards you. And the proof that Samuel is thus to be interpreted is shown by the following arrangements.

I note, in the first place, that although God expressly designated David, he still had to be elected by the people, who dutifully obeyed the will of God in choosing him. Solomon, similarly, was chosen first by God and then chosen again by the people.

And although the crown, by God's ordinance, was hereditary in the house of David, the people, as long as they were free, chose as they pleased among the children of a deceased king as we have said above.

Furthermore, in this procedure a twofold obligation was involved, as we see from the history of Joash. There was first an oath by which king and people obligated themselves to God in that they promised to observe His Law both ecclesiastical and political, and then a mutual oath between the king and the people. Then, do the people—that is, the estates of the people—have the right to correct the person they have elevated to dominion, if he does not do his duty? I say they have, and I put forward four examples. . . .

[After recalling the resistance of David to Saul and of Libnah to Jehoram, which involve resistance by inferior magistrates, the cases of Athaliah and of Amaziah are considered. There is a special effort to show that the killing of Amaziah was compatible with lawful procedure.

The survey of famous peoples then continues with examples from the history of the Danes, the Swedes, and the Scots.]

The English

As for the kingdom of England, it is the happiest in the world today, and may God please to keep it in tranquility. Although the crown is transmitted to the nearest of the princes of the blood, it is evident from several important histories, and most notably from the testimony of Polydore [Vergil] on the life of Henry I, that authority to rule is founded mostly on the consent of Parliament, as they call it. And surely the happy repose the English have enjoyed these many years under the mild and beneficent government of their most gracious Queen Elizabeth, as compared with the wretched and miserable condition of so many other countries, shows by experience what happiness and profit there is in moderation of royal power if it is rightly observed. God-fearing kings who love their peoples take guidance and advice that is offered to them with the obedience and reverence due their majesty. And they are not in this, allowing themselves to be governed by their subjects like a ward, as is claimed by the flatterers of princes, who eat of bread that is watered by the common people's tears, but are counselled and advised with the obedience and reverence due their majesty . . .

[Examples are given from Poland, Venice, and Spain. The long section on Spain deals first with various councils of the Spanish Church at which tyranny was condemned and then continues as follows.]

The Spanish

The other piece of evidence I promised to adduce is the formula still used in the Estates of Aragon (unless is has been recently changed) not only when they enthrone a king but at their regular meeting every third year. First, there are elaborate ceremonies between the person called the "Justice of Aragon," who represents the sovereignty to which the king must take an oath, and the person who is either about to be enthroned, or who already is the king and is appearing in his estates to do justice and to receive his due. Then this formula is pronounced: *Nos qui valemos tanto como vos, y podemos mas que vos, vos elegimos Rei con estas y estas conditiones, entra vos y nos un que manda mas qui vos;* that is, We who count as much as you, and who can do more than you, elect you king on these and these conditions, and between you and us there is one whose command is more than yours. This then is the way the Spaniards honored their kings—precisely as one should. . . .

[Examples are given from the Holy Roman Empire.]

The French

I come now to the Franks. Before their entry into Gaul, as Caesar shows us (in *De Bello Gallico, V*), the kings of their peoples were subject to the Estates, for there is a speech by Ambiorix of the Eburones in which he says, "Our laws are such that the people duly assembled have no less power over me than I have over them." And this is also clear from the speech of Vercingetorix, king of the Averni, defending his course before the assembly *(VII).**

The Gauls and the Franks were then united as the French,

*In this paragraph Gauls and Franks are inadvertently confused.

whose kingdom, unusually favored by God's providence, has long endured. But it is now so shaken, no matter whose the fault, that its ruin is greatly to be feared, for it is something that could hardly occur without bringing vast changes in a whole region of the world. I well understand that what I have to say will be taken well by some and ill by others. But since I shall be relating nothing but the facts, I am sure that God will sustain me against calumnies.

I say, then, that although the French chose their kings at first from the race of Merovée, then from the posterity of Charlemagne, and finally from the descendants of Hugh Capet, they so arranged their kingdom at the start that their kings did not reign by right of succession only, but were elected by consent of the Estates of the kingdom. Thus Pharamond was elected in 419, Pippin in 751, and his sons Charles and Carloman in 768, Charles inheriting his brother's share in 771 by the authority of the same assembly. And in 812 by its authority, he made his son Louis heir to his empire; and in his will—the text of which as given by Johannes Nauclerus is especially noteworthy and suffices of itself to decide the present question—he ordained that the people, *i.e.,* the Estates, should elect whichever of his children's sons they wished, and he commanded the uncles who might still survive to acquiesce in that election. And the oath taken in those days by the kings of France is reported by Aimon, who has Charles the Bold speak thus: "Since you have elected me to rule and govern you, know that it is my intention, with the help of God, to maintain the honor and service of God and His holy churches, and also to honor, protect, and honorably maintain each person in his rank and dignity to the best of my ability, and to insure each person in his privilege, right, and justice, in both ecclesiastical and secular affairs. I promise this so that the honor due the king, together with all due obedience as well as aid in maintaining and preserving the kingdom committed to my charge by God, shall be rendered to me by each of you according to his rank, dignity, and capacity as your ancestors justly, loyally, and reasonably promised."

And that these same Estates had the power to depose the

king they had elected in the event of misbehavior is evident
from many examples. Thus, in 461 Childeric was driven from
the throne for his insolence and robberies and replaced by
Gilo who was not of the Merovingian line. Chilperic was deposed in 578 and Theodoric in 667. In 890 the Estates passed
over the son of Charles the Bald and elected Eudes king. And
we read that Hugh Capet, in his effort to deprive Charles,
Lothar's brother of the throne, relied primarily on the long
record of Charles' misdeeds, hoping that the Estates would settle the whole dispute in the customary fashion. In brief, unless
the kingship was elective, the successions of both Pippin and
Hugh Capet were illegal, since there was no failure of male
heirs in the Merovingian line when Pippin became king, nor of
the Carolingian line when Capet obtained possession of the
throne.

The authority of the Estates to appoint and to depose the
chief officers of the crown, or at least to supervise the king in
this, as well as their authority to impose taxes and to deal
with all the main affairs of government in peace and war, is
equally clear. There is abundant evidence in old and reliable
histories that clearly reveals the shamelessness of those sycophants who seek their fortune in the destruction of a kingdom
so well ordered. In the France of our day, the closest male
relative of a king succeeds to the throne without a meeting of
the Estates, and everything is turned upside down at the whim
of those who have entered his good graces. The Estates are no
longer assembled at regular intervals but are called at the
pleasure of individuals who are concerned only with their own
profit and security. And they are convoked not to make decisions but simply to hear speeches, which are meant not to inform but to distract, while the decisions are left to the very
persons who are the principal targets of complaint. In short,
wars are declared and peace concluded, taxes are levied and
loans authorized, laws both in public and private matters are
passed or repealed, dignities and offices are conferred or taken
away—all at the pleasure of particular persons, who may be
male or female, noble or mean, upright or debased, as long
as they remain in the good graces of masters who see only

through their eyes and hear only through their ears. Such practices are completely contrary to the good old customs of our ancestors, and directly contradict the fundamental laws of the French kingdom established at the time of its foundation.

I leave it to any jurist of learning and good conscience to decide whether any prescription of time, however long, applies to matters of this sort by any law divine or human. And yet, even to this day our kings take an oath at their anointment (which should be publicized and known throughout the world). They are also required, upon their accession, to confirm the privileges of towns and of officers of the kingdom (even though there are many abuses of this custom). And if the king is a minor, the Estates decide who will administer the kingdom.

All these rights of the estates are remnants of that authority of old that is disappearing bit by bit. It is not yet 200 years since the Estates, in 1380, disallowed the testament of Charles V, surnamed the Wise. And as recently as 1467, Louis XI, who turned the French monarchy into a tyranny so far as he was able (an alteration described by court sycophants as freeing kings from tutelage), was rightly charged with maladministration of the kingdom by the Estates assembled at Tours [1468] and assigned thirty-six guardians to oversee his conduct. It is true that this king, who made a mockery of every oath and promise (using as his pretext the good Lady of Cléry), was able to get around this. Yet it was to his own disadvantage and unhappiness. Even apart from his infamy, which continues to this day, he found no peace while he lived; and even at the point of death he had reason to regret that he was more feared than loved by his subjects.

And on the importance of keeping oaths, I shall here mention another very memorable example. Charles VII, then still Dauphin and badly advised, had John, the last Duke of Burgundy, descended from the royal line of France, brutally murdered before his very eyes despite the oath of peace and friendship sworn between them but a short time earlier near Melun. Duke John richly merited this, God's judgment. But the perjury involved cost France a million souls and the devastation of most of its territory. And King Charles, whom his father disinherited, was to see his enemy crowned king of France at Paris, while Charles was king less of France than of the town of Bourges. Charles finally bought peace through the Treaty of Arras, but only at a heavy price. Even though he treated with Philip, Duke of Burgundy and son of John, as king with vassal, the following clause was inserted in the treaty. "The king," it says, "shall assent and affix his seal to this—that if this treaty should subsequently be broken by him, his vassals, followers, and subjects, present and future, will no longer be obligated to obey and serve him but will instead be obligated to obey the Duke of Burgundy and his successors. In that case all vassals, subjects, and servants will be absolved and freed of all oaths of fealty and all other promises and obligations of service by which they may have been bound to King Charles, with no further liability or claim against them in the future. And King Charles now and henceforth orders this and frees and discharges them from every oath and obligation, should the aforementioned case arise." This was the outcome of the violation of an oath by a king who had been badly counselled. Yet because that agreement was observed, the kingdom found repose. And if it was reasonable to add that clause, which was only a supplementary promise and not a fundamental condition of the king's administration, shall we have less respect for the promise and condition on which a king is [initially] accepted by his people, and which is based, indeed, on a principle of equity and natural reason; his promise, that is, to govern according to the law of which he is supposed to be the sovereign protector?

The conclusion, therefore, is that sovereign governance is granted to kings or other sovereign magistrates with the proviso that if they depart from the good laws and conditions they have sworn to uphold and become notorious tyrants who are unwilling to take good advice, it is the right of lesser magistrates to provide for themselves and those within their care by resisting flagrant tyranny. And the Estates of the country, or a similar body, to whom such authority is given by law, can and should resist until good order is restored and may, if need be, punish the tyrant according to his crimes. In so acting, they are in no sense mutineers or rebels, but are simply doing their sworn duty to God and to their country.

Arguments from General Maxims

And although we have proved this by clear examples drawn from ancient as well as modern kingdoms and empires, I shall now advance arguments from reason so that no one may object that the question should be decided by precepts, not examples.

I assert, then, that equity and natural law, on which all human society depends, permit no doubt on the following two points. First, in all agreements based solely on the consent of the contracting parties, the obligation may be broken by those who made it for sufficient cause—from which it follows that they who have the power to create a king also have the power to depose him. Second, if there is any just occasion to dissolve a contract or agreement—an occasion, that is, when the obligation nullifies itself—it is when there has been a flagrant violation of the essential condition in consideration of which the obligation was contracted.

Let them, therefore, who so exalt the authority of sovereigns as to dare say that no matter what kings do they have no other judge than God, prove to me that there ever was a nation so unmindful of its interests as to submit itself—knowingly and without intimidation or constraint—to the will of a sovereign, without attaching the condition, expressed or implied, that they must be justly and equitably governed. And if examples are advanced of conquered peoples who have subjected themselves to all the conditions demanded by their conquerors, I shall not, with the jurists, depend only on the answer that a promise extorted by force or intimidation is invalid (since I admit that theology, the rule of conscience, does not permit even an obligation of this sort to be violated lightly). I will say, rather, that even if a people knowingly, and in complete freedom, has consented to something that is in itself manifestly irreligious and contrary to the law of nature, the obligation is invalid—which is to remove all doubt as to its invalidity when it has been extorted by force or by intimidation, or has been entered into through obvious ignorance or fraud. For this universal rule of justice, based on maxims and common principles that have remained in man despite his fall, is so definite and firm that nothing clearly contrary and repugnant to it should be found proper and valid among men. I am referring here to things so clearly irreligious and iniquitous that no one not completely void of sense would deny that such things can neither be asked nor complied with in good conscience. . . .

[Several examples are advanced.]

But suppose that a people—either through foolishness, or blandishments, or because they have had a good prince and presume his offspring will be like him—have submitted to someone absolutely and without express condition. Shall we say that this prince may do anything he pleases, or must we not imply, as if expressed, conditions which are in their nature, holy and in accordance with the law? If not, then how shall we survive, and what will be the life of men, if this prince were to kill his mother and his father, and violate young girls and women, and pillage and massacre subjects at his whim, on the pretext that the people, trusting the probity of that prince, accepted him without condition?

And it would surely be monstrously unfair to deny to an entire nation what equity concedes to private persons such as minors, women, and the simpleminded, as well as to those who have been cheated in a bargain by more than half the just price—especially where the damage to these persons seems to result from the bad faith of the party who is benefited. Is there anyone whose faith is worse than a tyrant so brazen as to claim a right to all things right or wrong because he obtained this right by contract with his people, or received such power from his forebears? I assert, then, (as I have said at length before) that the Estates, or a body similarly ordained, should interpose their power nonetheless, although it is illicit for private persons to take the public initiative upon themselves, or for lesser magistrates to exceed the limits of their station.

I ask, further, whether the obligation of a subject to his king is greater than that of a child to his father, of a slave to his master, or of a freedman to his patron (as the Romans called the person who emancipated him). Let us listen, to begin with, to what Cicero justly and reasonably says about the duty of a son towards a father who would forcibly usurp dominion in his country. "If a father," he says, "attempts to seize power or betray his country, shall his son keep silent? No. He will rather beg his father not to do it. If this does not succeed, he will accuse him publicly and will even threaten him; and if it finally comes to the point where the ruin of his country threatens, he will put the life of his father second to his country's safety." Hence, then, is an opinion in conformity with reason from a person of no slight authority. And as for slaves: under Roman law a slave was considered free if his master did not provide for him. Even more significant, the slave, under Roman law, was entitled to denounce his master in a case of treason. And who is more culpable of treason than a tyrant openly violating all law human and divine? But before whom can he be indicted, you will ask? Before those, I answer, who, since they had the power to create him, also have the power to judge him; and who are the principal protectors of the sovereignty and its ultimate guardians, from whose verdict there is no appeal. Similarly, a freedman, although bound to show reverence to his patron and ordinarily unable to appear as a party against him in a civil suit, is nevertheless permitted under Roman law to bring criminal action if the patron has inflicted serious personal injury or has had adulterous relations with the freedman's wife. I use these arguments not to suggest that [Roman] civil law or the opinion of this or that philosopher should be taken as a rule of conscience, but only to show the manifest unreason of that opinion which allows no lawful way to halt flagrant tyranny, no matter how iniquitous or cruel.

And the saying that the king is not subject to the law is surely not to be taken generally, as all the flatterers of kings and destroyers of kingdoms chant in unison. Not to mention the many examples to the contrary put forward above from the history of all nations, how shall we account for the celebrated maxims of the ancient jurists, which they have founded on the law of nature? They say, for example, that he who makes the laws should obey them; that there is nothing more conducive to authority than to live according to the law; that it is an expression worthy of a prince to avow that he is bound by law. And if the jurists sometimes seem to say that the king is above the law, they are to be understood as referring only to civil laws dealing with particular private relations such as the Trebellian or Falcidian deductions in the law of legacies, not to public law or matters relating to the state, and even less to divine and natural law by which every single man is bound by the very fact that he is born a man. It therefore follows either that kings are not men, or else that they are subject to this law.

But suppose it be objected that public law, which relates to the state of a people or a nation (for it is of this that we are speaking), is different from a law of nature that is common to all peoples. I admit that there are certain differences but hold that these depend on special circumstances, which is not to deny a general and universal rule of equity and rectitude so firm that a government that goes against it—which approves obvious irreligion, robberies, and other things notoriously opposed to God, the law of nature, and good custom—must be repudiated and condemned.

Another possible objection is that although a sovereign who acts otherwise than I have said is surely guilty, he has no other judge but God. And the case of David will perhaps be cited, who committed a nefarious murder as well as adultery, and yet was never judged by any human being. I answer, first, that as is evident from all that has been said before, peoples and Estates have ordinarily reserved the power of restraining sovereigns, which reservation cannot be prejudiced by disuse however long, or by any prescription of time. I say, second, that there is a great difference between doing occasional harm in a restricted number of cases and abandonment to evil as a way of life, which is like the difference between a prince whose private life is vicious and one who overthrows every rule of justice in his government. But although I do not say that a sovereign should be treated like one of his subjects for private and strictly personal vices, I would yet say that even these can become so flagrant that he may and must be halted. All the more reason then, when public order is at stake, for those so authorized to act, if they are not to violate their oaths to God and to their country. If these distinctions are applied to the life of David as a whole, and if the satisfaction that he offered publicly for his crime is borne in mind, it will not seem strange that no further action was taken against him. And besides, it does not follow that a person who escapes punishment does not deserve it. . . .

[No valid objection may be derived from the examples of the Turkish monarchy, which is declared inhuman and illegitimate.

The lapse of obligation to a tyrant-king is compared with the suspension of the marital obligations of a wife under certain conditions.]

Furthermore, since the kingdoms and even empires are fiefs, owing homage and service to the sovereignty, we may argue from the law of fiefs. Book 2, title 26, paragraph 24, and title 47 [of the *Libri feudorum*] hold that a lord may commit felony against his vassal, just as a vassal may, against his lord. It is true that in the former case the fief of the lord reverts not to his vassal but to the principal of whom he holds, yet it is clear enough that the lord committing felony always forfeits all his claims upon the vassal. I conclude, then, that in the situation we are here considering, a king or even an emperor, by virtue of the fact that he holds of the sovereignty itself, loses his fief if—may it never come to pass—he commits felony against his vassals, *i.e.,* his subjects, although that fief is not awarded to these vassals individually but reverts to those who represent the sovereignty so that they may provide a new possessor. And the full force of this argument appears when we consider that when a vassal invests subvassals of his own, he does not take an oath to these expressly, so that the aforementioned rule on the crime of felony against one's vassal depends solely on natural equity and does not have to be mentioned expressly. Hence, the force of the rule is even greater when a ruler commits felony against his subjects, to whom he is bound by an explicit oath. Moreover, even supposing that the lord could not lose his fief for felony against the vassal, the fief of the vassal is clearly forfeited for felony against his lord. But the emperor himself, as we have shown, owes homage to the empire of which he is the chief and sovereign vassal, and this applies as much or even more to the position of kings with respect to their kingdoms. Hence, there can be no doubt that their fiefs are forfeited if they commit felony so extreme as to become notorious and incorrigible tyrants, which rule, as we have shown, has everywhere been practiced.

And the more sensible part of those who call themselves Roman Catholics agree, on the basis both of reason and examples, that the Ecumenical Council is above the Pope and has the power to depose him, at least for the crime of heresy. Hence, it follows either that kings have more authority than Popes and that heresy is a lesser crime than tyranny, or else that a people has as much power over a tyrant-king as a Council over a heretic Pope.

VII. What remedies are available if a tyrant prevents the Estates from meeting?

This is my opinion, then, on the rights of subjects of various degrees against a sovereign who has become a notorious tyrant. But there is still another question of no slight difficulty. What is to be done if tyranny has become so entrenched that action by the Estates is difficult to obtain owing to the connivance, fear, or wickedness of the majority or of the leaders? To private persons, who have not been authorized either by the lesser magistrates or by the more sober part of the Estates (about which I shall speak directly), my answer is that they have no other remedy but penitence and patience joined with prayers, which God will not disdain and without which any other remedy, no matter how lawful it may be, involves the danger of God's curse. But this does not prevent private persons from going to the lesser magistrates and asking them to do their duty. And when the lesser magistrates, or the more sober part of them, enlist the aid of private persons, the duty of the latter to God and to their country is clear from what has gone before. As for the lesser magistrates, it is for them to join together and press for a convocation of the Estates, while defending themselves against flagrant tyranny insofar as they can and to the extent they should. Finally, it is the duty of each estate to seek a common and lawful assembly—one in which the wicked will not obstruct the good, nor the cowardly hold back the zealous, nor the majority restrain the men of better judgment. Moreover, I say that, in an emergency like this, it is the obligation of private citizens to follow the lesser magistrates, which is the duty of a subject, and that it is even permissible for the more sober part of them to seek aid from foreigners, if need be, and especially from friends and allies of the kingdom.

In confirmation of this I shall advance some examples that are well acknowledged. . . .

[Four examples follow, two from the Old Testament, one from Roman history, and another, concerning Charlemagne, from French history.]

I think, then, that my position [in favor of resisting tyranny] is sufficiently established, assuming always that the following conditions are met: that the tyranny has become thoroughly obvious; that there is no recourse to arms until all other remedies have been tried; and that there is careful consideration not only of what is permitted but of what is expedient, lest the cure be worse than the disease.

It remains, in concluding this treatise, to answer the principal objections, omitting those I have already dealt with in passing. . . .

[The response to objections is for the most part a restatement of the main theses.

Magistrates, it is conceded, are established to rule, but only in accordance with divine and human justice.

Subjects should no doubt be patient toward a tyrant, but only with the limitations and distinctions established in the treatise.

David's patience with Saul is most commendable, but it does not prove that there are no lawful occasions for armed resistance.

Zedekiah's punishment for revolt against the Chaldeans does not argue against the general principle since God had explicitly ordered the subjection of the Jews to the Chaldeans.

The prayers of the Jews for Nebuchadnezzar are explained by the same exception. Not only were they private persons, but they were also enslaved to Nebuchadnezzar by God's express command.

The objection that tyrannies occur by God's will and should therefore be borne patiently has already been answered. Legitimate self-defense against a tyrant, as against any criminal, is permissible unless God has expressly demanded the contrary. For although all things happen by God's will, His providence cannot be anticipated in a specific situation unless it has been expressly revealed. In the absence of such revelation, one must act according to God's general commands.

The revolt of the Israelites against Rehoboam w⌐s justly condemned, even though Rehoboam was clearly a tyrant. But the condemnation was only because the Israelites proceeded in an unlawful manner.

The commandments of St. Peter and St. Paul to pray for rulers who were tyrants do not mean that prayer is the exclusive remedy (except for private citizens). Even then there may be prayers or imprecations against the tyrant, like those authorized against Julian the Apostate by the Church of that time.

Jesus Christ paid tribute to Tiberius, who was a usurper in Judea as well as a tyrant. But this is because Jesus Christ, renouncing his prerogatives, wished to appear as a private citizen. In addition, the Roman usurpation in Judea had by that time been accepted.]

VIII. May princes be resisted for unjust taxation?

Suppose we are asked about a prince who oppresses his people with unjust taxes and subsidies. After remonstrations have been made, those having authority may and should restore order according to the laws of the realm, as we have indicated. But this also should be noted: a prince who exceeds his power in a matter like this should not be hastily judged a tyrant simply because he is extravagant, greedy, or given to some other vice. Tyranny implies confirmed wickedness involving general subversion of the political order and of the fundamental laws of a realm. I further say that even where there is just occasion for forcible resistance to tyranny, this important maxim should be kept in mind (even though it was a pagan who enunciated it), namely, that wise men explore things very carefully before they take up arms. . . .

IX. *May subjects make agreements with their princes?*

I must also answer those who think it wrong for subjects to make agreements with a [ruling] sovereign. What are their arguments? If reason is the test, I can think of no sufficient ground. They say that it is for subjects to take orders from the king, not the reverse; that subjects, therefore, may express grievances to their prince with all due reverence and may give their advice when it is asked, but they may not go any further. Subjects, I reply, should surely not approach their supreme or lesser magistrates except with honor and reverence, and not only for fear of provoking them to wrath but for conscience's sake, as the Apostle teaches us, since their position is ordained by God. Yet I deny that the above conclusion necessarily follows from this rule, as if, in matters of public order, after explaining to the sovereign, with all due reverence, the course of action demanded by reason and by justice and also by the conditions under which he was raised to his position, one must necessarily put up with anything the sovereign may please to do and forego all further remedy. I say, rather, that in this situation it is not unjust to lead him back into the path of duty and even to take stronger measure if reason proves of no avail. In short, the king received his administration under definite conditions, and no new agreement is imposed on him if he is required either to observe the original conditions or else to make way for someone who will keep them better. And if examples are wanted, I think the ones I gave earlier are enough to discredit the maxim that the mere will of a king should always be enough for subjects, since this is founded neither on reason nor on any usage of well-ordered monarchies.

X. *May force be used to resist religious persecution?*

It remains only to resolve an issue of the greatest consequence. Where there is tyranny in matters of religion, may persecution be resisted by force of arms according to the above distinctions and conditions? The principal objection here is that since religion is a matter of conscience, which may not be coerced, it should not be established by arms. And indeed we see that it has rather been advanced by the preaching of God's Word and by prayers and patience, to which are added those passages of Scripture that indicate the difference between the kingdom of this world and the kingdom of the spirit. And beyond this we are given the example of the faithful prophets and of Jesus Christ Himself, who, although all authority, force, and power belonged to Him, abstained from force completely, as did the ancient martyrs afterwards, so that there were even legions, complete and fully armed, who suffered death without drawing the sword.

I answer, to begin with, that it is utterly absurd and false to say that worldly methods of resistance, such as appeal to courts or resort to arms, are not only different from spiritual resistance, but are also so opposed and repugnant to it that they can have no place whatsoever in religious matters. On the contrary, the chief duty of a good magistrate is to employ all the means that God has given him to make sure that God is recognized and served as king of kings by the subjects whom God has committed to his care. To this end, accordingly, he should use the weapon of the law against disturbers of the true religion who will not listen to the admonitions and censures of the Church and his military arm against those who cannot otherwise be halted.

In corroboration of this there are both good reasons and express authority of Scripture. The argument from reason is that the true end of all rightly ordered government is not tranquility in this life, as certain pagan philosophers have thought, but the glory of God, to which all of our present life should be directed. Hence, the governors of peoples should use all the means God gave them to maintain God's service (in which His glory lies) among those committed to their care. And even if peace in this life were the final end of government, it would still have to be admitted that the true way of maintaining and preserving peace is to serve Him who is its giver and preserver. . . .

[References to Scripture follow on the obligation of promoting true religion. It is noted that the earliest Councils against heretics were summoned under the authority of the emperors and that this responsibility of rulers has been constantly recognized ever since.]

But what, then, is the relevance of this long discussion of the duty of kings and magistrates to maintain religion for deciding whether they may be forcibly resisted if they persecute it? I reply that it is one thing to introduce religion in a country, another to preserve it once it is established or to restore it when it has been buried, as it were, under the connivance, ignorance, and wickedness of men. I hold, then, that religion is planted and increased by the Spirit of God alone, through the Word, which is ordained for teaching, encouraging, and exhorting, since this is the special activity of the Holy Spirit, which works by spiritual means. The duty of a prince who would convert his subjects from idolatry or superstition to true religion is to see that they are given good and lively instruction, while the duty of subjects, correspondingly, is to yield to reason and to truth. The prince, finally, should provide and enforce good edicts against those who, from pure stubbornness, would resist establishment of the true religion, as has been done in our time in England, Denmark, Sweden, Scotland, and in a large part of Germany and of Switzerland, against Papists, Anabaptists, and other heretics. And if, instead of believing in the bloodstained whore of Rome, other nations had done likewise, there would be peace not only in religion but in all other public matters, too.

But what may subjects do if there is an attempt to force idolatry upon their conscience? Any effort to force the prince to alter established public order would surely be entirely wrong. They should rather endure persecution patiently while continuing to serve God, or else go into exile. But if there are edicts, lawfully passed and promulgated by public authority, permitting exercise of the true religion, then the prince, I maintain, is even more bound to respect these than any other law since the religious order is of greater consequence than any other, and he may not repeal them at his own initiative and discretion. If he does, he is guilty of flagrant tyranny, to which opposition is permitted according to the distinctions previously laid down, and with all the better reason in that our souls and our consciences ought to be more precious to us than all the goods of this world.

Hence, it should cause no surprise that Jesus Christ, the prophets, the Apostles, and the other martyrs remained, as private persons, within the bounds of their station. And as for those magistrates, and those entire legions together with their leaders who suffered martyrdom without resisting, even though their persecutors were violating previously established edicts in favor of the Christians—most cases of this sort occurring under Diocletian and Julian—I have a twofold answer. First, even though emperors before Diocletian, such as Hadrian, Antoninus, and Alexander, softened the persecutions, they had not permitted public exercise of the Christian religion. Second, not everything licit is expedient, and I do not hold that where religion is authorized by law, it must always be defended against open tyranny by force of arms. But that this can be done in good conscience by those with appropriate authority when God has given them the means is attested by the example of Libnah against Jehoram, of Jerusalem against Amaziah, and the war of Constantine against Maxentius at the request of the city of Rome, all of which have been cited. And I thus conclude that we must honor as martyrs not only those who have conquered without resistance, and by patience only, against tyrants who have persecuted the truth, but those also who, authorized by law and by competent authorities, devoted their strength to the defense of true religion. . . .

Part III

Vindiciae contra tyrannos

Editor's Note

The *Vindiciae contra tyrannos*[1] was published pseudonymously at Basel in 1579, and the question of its authorship is still not definitely settled.[2] The basic difficulty is a conflict in the documentary record. There is one tradition pointing to Hubert Languet, a diplomatic agent for the Elector of Saxony, and another pointing to Philippe du Plessis-Mornay, who was Languet's younger and devoted friend. But the sources in favor of Mornay ultimately depend on the testimony of Mornay himself, whereas those in favor of Languet go back to a manuscript of the *Vindiciae* written in his hand, which was seen by scholars after Languet died. Hence, if one had to choose between the two, Mornay would be considered as the author and the Languet autograph would be explained by his participation, at one stage or another, in preparing the work for publication.[3]

In recent years, however, a number of scholars, but by no means all, have tended to believe that the *Vindiciae* was a collaborative effort and have assigned question 3 to Languet, the other three questions to Mornay, who is supposed to have put the whole together. The argument, made by G. T. van Ysselsteyn[4] in 1931, is too complicated to be recapitulated here. But a few observations may be offered.

The argument, first of all, is unconvincing. Almost everything depends on showing that Question 3 was once a separate treatise in view of its theme, its sources, and its style. But the style and sources follow fairly closely from the theme, so that the latter is the crucial issue. And the theme of Question 3, which deals with secular resistance, is closely related to the questions of resistance on religious grounds in Question 2. Indeed, both topics are also taken up as separate but related questions in the *Right of Magistrates,* which we know was written by one man. The organization of the *Vindiciae* is therefore natural enough in its time. All we are left with are certain minor peculiarities in Question 3, which can be accounted for in many ways. They are surely not sufficient to establish dual authorship in the absence of documentary evidence.[5]

Second, the argument is imprecise as to its grounds. It is often difficult to tell whether van Ysselsteyn is arguing from all of question 3 or only that rather small and insignificant part of it that deals with the portrait of a tyrant. His imprecision is instructive, since it shows that the effort to find traces of Languet in the *Vindiciae* is highly speculative.

The entire issue, finally, is not particularly significant. It is not suggested that the interpretation of the substance of Question 3 would change if Languet were taken as its author, or even that minor points of doctrine would be clarified. Even on van Ysselsteyn's account, the work is best understood as Mornay's responsibility since he is still supposed to have written most of the *Vindiciae* and to have put the work together with great care.

My own inclination, therefore, is to look upon Mornay as the author without ruling out collaboration.* Languet may have undertaken to edit the *Vindiciae* at one point or another. In the five years that elapsed between the time the work was begun and the date of publication, he may have inspired, influenced, and even helped Mornay in ways we can no longer specify. Mornay, indeed, may well have wished to represent the thought of many men. Pierre Loyseleur de Villiers may well have influenced the final product since Grotius names him as the man who prepared it for the printer.[6] We may also note that all three men collaborated in the drafting of William of Orange's *Apology* against the ban of Phillip II of Spain, which reflects certain themes to be found in the *Vindiciae.*

Philippe du Plessis-Mornay (1549–1623) came from a distinguished noble family. He was well educated, widely travelled, intellectually curious, and highly effective as a publicist. But unlike Hotman and Beza, he was neither an academic nor pastor by profession, but rather a diplomat and soldier, who played a leading role in reorganizing the Huguenot party after the decimation of 1573. Despite his youth, he was named counsellor to Henry of Navarre in 1576 and became one of his most influential political advisers. Mornay's political strategy was to rally the moderates of France against the extremism of the Catholic League. In Mornay's larger scheme, the national goals of France were to be linked to the support of the Netherlands revolt and to the formation of an alliance that would counterbalance the power of Spain in Europe. On both these points, he was a persuasive

---

*These conclusions, reached by traditional methods, are supported by the statistical work of Graham Jagger ("On the Authorship of the *Vindiciae contra tyrannos,*" *Durham University Journal,* March 1968, pp. 73–80) of which I was unaware at the time the above was written. After studying the sentence length characteristics of the four parts of the *Vindiciae,* Jagger concludes that all were most probably written by one man (p. 76). And after comparing the characteristic sentence lengths of the *Vindiciae* with the characteristics of works known to be written by Languet and by Mornay, he concludes that the *Vindiciae* probably could not have been written by the former but could have been written by the latter (p. 77).

advocate of strategic conceptions shared widely by members of the Huguenot movement.

On religious questions Mornay, like Languet,[7] was consistently in favor of religious toleration. But he remained a militant Protestant even at the cost of straining relations with Henry after the latter's reconversion to Catholicism. In 1600 he withdrew from court to attend his post as governor of Saumur, which he continued to hold when Henry died. But in 1620, after a Protestant uprising, which he had apparently attempted to discourage, he was deprived of his office and his pension; and he retired to his estate, where he died in 1623. Despite his close connection to the complicated politics of the time, he is presented by all of his biographers as a model of personal integrity both in his public and his private life.[8]

The present translation is based on the Latin text of 1579, shortened according to the same policy indicated for the *Right of Magistrates*. The only point that need be noted is that Questions 2 and 4 have been somewhat under-represented because they are less concerned with the central questions of constitutionalism and resistance.

A complete translation of the *Vindiciae*, made in 1648 and reprinted in 1689, is still available in recent reprint.[9] The old translation, however, is archaic in its style and language and is often misleadingly free. Moreover, it is often erroneous and negligent, and it has not been corrected for typographical mistakes.

Jo: Bander

VINDICIAE,
CONTRA TY
RANNOS:

SIVE,

DE PRINCIPIS IN
Populum, Populíque in Princi-
pem, legitima potestate,

STEPHANO IVNIO
Bruto Celta, Auctore.

[Languet, Hubert]

[Du Plessis-Marnay]?

EDIMBVRGI, AN-
NO M. D. LXXIX.

Vindiciae contra tyrannos

The First Question

Are subjects bound to obey princes if their orders contradict the Law of God?

At first sight this question may seem utterly idle and profitless, since it implies that uncertainty exists about an indubitable axiom of Christianity, which is stated very frequently in Holy Scripture, which has been exemplified continuously throughout the centuries, and which has been attested by the pyres of many martyrs. For why, it may be asked, have the faithful endured so many painful trials if they did not all believe that only God is to be obeyed absolutely and implicitly—kings, on the other hand, only insofar as their commands are not in conflict with God's Law? Or how are we to interpret the maxims of the Apostles that we are to obey God rather than men? And since only the will of the one God is invariably just and injustice is always possible in the will of every other being, how can we doubt that our obedience to God must be implicit and that our obedience to men must always be conditional? Yet there are princes today, professing to be Christians, who brazenly arrogate a power so unlimited that it cannot be from God at all; and they have a swarm of flatterers, who worship them as gods on earth and who, from fear or other pressure, believe, or pretend to believe, that there is no occasion in which princes ought not to be obeyed. The vice of our times, it thus appears, is that there is nothing so firm as to pass uncontradicted, or so certain as to pass undoubted, or so sacred as to go unviolated. Hence anyone who reflects on the matter will conclude, I fear, that this question is not only useful but even highly necessary, especially in our age. . . .

[One should obey God rather than man. God is the proprietor

of all, men are only usufructuaries of their possessions. The relationship of kings to God may be compared to that of vassals to their lords. The vassal's fief is forfeited for felony, *i.e.,* for breach of faith.]

In short, if the vassal does not keep the fealty he swore, his fief is forfeited and he is legally deprived of all prerogatives. So also with the king. If he neglects God, if he goes over to His enemies and is guilty of felony towards God, his kingdom is forfeited of right and is often lost in fact. And this principle is clearly shown in the covenant that is regularly concluded between the king and God (for God sees fit to honor His servants by accepting them as partners to a covenant). At the coronation of kings, then, we read of a twofold covenant: the first, between God, the king, and the people that the people will be God's people; the second, between the king and the people that if he is a proper ruler, he will be obeyed accordingly. We will consider the second of these later and here take up the first.

The Covenant Between God and the King

We read that at the coronation of Joash a covenant was concluded between God, the king, and the people—or, as it is related elsewhere, between the high priest Jehoiada, the whole people, and the king—that they would be God's people; and in yet another place that Josiah and the whole people entered into a covenant with God. We also learn that in making this covenant the high priest, speaking in God's name, expressly asked the king and the people, first, whether they were willing to guarantee that God would be purely worshipped in the Jewish kingdom according to His ritual; second, whether the king, in ruling, would permit the people to serve God and also hold them to God's Law; and finally, whether the people in obeying the king would obey God no less and first of all. Thus the king and the people, like joint underwriters of a promise, swore to keep the Law of God, and obliged themselves by solemn oath to worship God above all. Hence, as soon as this covenant was solemnized, Josiah and Joash extirpated the idolatrous cult of Baal and restored the service of God.

The articles of this covenant were, in sum, as follows: the king and the entire people would worship God according to the prescription of His Law as individuals and would act collectively to protect that worship; that if they did so, God would be with them and preserve their commonwealth. If not, he would despise and abandon them. And this is evident from a great many passages in Scripture. . . .

[Cases from the Old Testament are cited in which kings lost their kingdoms because they broke their oath to God.]

But since the form of the church and the kingdom of the Jews has changed, and what was formerly bounded by Judea has spread throughout the world, we should now consider Christian kings. Just as the Gospels succeeded to the Law, Christian rulers have replaced the Jewish kings. The covenant remains the same; the stipulations are unaltered; and there are the same penalties if these are not fulfilled, as well as the same God, omnipotent, avenging perfidy. And as the Jews were bound to keep the Law, so are Christians to observe the Gospels, and each Christian is sworn to propagation of the Gospels as his first and chief concern. . . .

[Warning is given to contemporary kings who persecute Protestant defenders of the true religion.]

What, then, of heathen kings? Although not anointed by God, they are undoubtedly His vassals, and have received their power from Him alone, whether by lot or any other means. For if by vote, it is God who rules the hearts of men and guides them to the one He wills. And if by lot, it is thrown into the midst, says Solomon, and sorted out by God. It is always by Him only, and by His judgment, that kings are raised up, established, confirmed, and overthrown. For which reason Isaiah calls Cyrus the "anointed of the Lord," and Daniel, also, says that Nebuchadnezzar and the rest received their power from God, which is what [St.] Paul says of any magistrate whatever. For although God did not entrust His Law to them expressly, they acknowledge that they owe their reign to God, the highest king. Hence, if they do not see that the tribute owed to God is paid or, even worse, if they divert and seize what is due God from His proper subjects, or arrogate divine jurisdiction to themselves in any other way, it is truly a crime of the kingdom so affected, for which God has grievously punished even pagan kings. . . .

[The principle of rendering unto Caesar what is Caesar's and unto God what is God's is restated in several formulations, and additional examples and analogies are given. The principle is then established by citation of authorities, including the First Table of the Law, which is even more sacred than the Second.]

But on this matter, we are not without an express law stated in specific terms. Whenever the Christian apostles enjoin obedience to kings and magistrates, they take special pains to warn us that we must obey God first of all, so they do not provide the slightest ground for that preposterous servility that the sycophants of princes urge upon the simpleminded. "Let every soul," says [St.] Paul, "be subject to the higher powers, for there is no power but of God." (He says "every soul" so that no rank may seek exemption.) These words are enough to make it clear that we are to obey God before the king, that we obey the king because of God and surely not against Him. But wishing to avoid all ambiguity, he adds that the prince is God's minister for our good and to do justly—from which we may again conclude that we are to obey God rather than His minister. But even this, he thought, was not enough. Render, he says, tribute to whom tribute is due; honor, to whom honor is due; reverence, to whom reverence is due; as if to say, with Christ, render unto Caesar what is Caesar's, unto God what is God's. . . .

[Consideration of the first question concludes with further citations of authority, elaborations, and reformulations.]

The Second Question

Is it permissible to resist a prince who violates God's Law and desolates His Church? Who may resist, in what manner, and to what extent?

. . . The question here is whether it is permissible to resist a prince who is a violator of God's Law and is trying either to destroy His Church or to obstruct its propagation. Holy Scripture, if only we accept its verdict, will provide us with an answer. For if, as may readily be shown, the Jewish people taken as a whole were not only so permitted but enjoined, none, I believe, will deny that the same must surely apply to the whole people of a Christian kingdom.

The prime consideration here is that God, in choosing the Jews from all the other nations as His chosen people, made a covenant with them that they would be God's people, which is documented throughout the Book of Deuteronomy. . . . Hence, we see that the whole people was obligated to maintain God's Law, to defend His Church, and thus to drive the idols of the gentiles from the Land of Canaan, which stipulation cannot apply to individuals, but only to the people as a whole. And it is significant, in this respect, that all the tribes encamped around the Ark of the Lord, so that what was entrusted to the care of all all were obliged to protect. . . .

[Examples are given of collective action taken by the Jews to punish violations of God's Law.]

The Covenant Between God and the People

When kings were given to the people, this compact did not lapse but was instead confirmed and constantly renewed. We have said that at the coronation of a king a twofold covenant was made. The first was between God, the king, and the people. (Indeed, the people are put first in *Chronicles* 2:23.) And its purpose was that the people should become God's people, that is, that they should be God's Church. Why God covenanted with the king we have already shown; why, with the whole people we must now inquire. For its is certain that God did not require this in vain. And it would have been an empty covenant if there were not some authority remaining in the people to make a promise and to keep it. It seems, therefore, that God did what creditors so often do with borrowers of doubtful credit, which is to obligate several for the same amount so that there are two or more co-signers for the single loan, each one of whom may be held responsible for the entire sum as though he were the principal debtor. Since it was dangerous to entrust the Church to a single, all-too-human individual, the Church was committed and entrusted to the people as a whole. The king, situated on a slippery height, could easily have fallen into irreligion. Hence, God wished to have the people intervene, so that the Church might not be ruined with the king.

In the stipulation we are now discussing, God, or the high priest acting as His representative, is the stipulating party; the king and the people as a whole—that is, Israel—are the promissory parties, both being conjointly obligated of their own accord for one and the same thing. The high priest asks the people whether they will promise to become God's people and to assume the obligation of maintaining His Temple and His Church among them, wherein He will be duly worshipped. Then the king gives his promise, and the people give their promise (the corporate body of them here acting as a single individual). And it is clear, from the very wording of their oaths, that these promises are given conjointly, and not separately, at the same and not at different times. The king and Israel, therefore, are established as two co-signers equally obligated for the entire promise. And just as Caius and Titus, who have jointly promised Seius the same stipulated sum of money, are each individually bound by law for the entire sum, and the whole may be demanded of either one of them; so the king, on his part, and the people, on their part, are bound to see that no harm is suffered by the Church. If one of them is negligent, God may demand the whole from either, and from the people sooner than the king, since many men are less likely to default than one and have more resources. . . . So, if Israel turns away from God and the king does not correct them, the guilt of the people falls on him. Conversely, if the king goes over to false gods and not only goes over but takes others with him and seeks to destroy the Church in every way he can; and if Israel fails to drag him back from this defection, by use of force if necessary, then his guilt falls on them. . . .

[Examination of the Biblical accounts shows that the Covenant did in fact anticipate that kings would be corrected by the people.]

For how can we understand why the consent of the whole people was required, why they were constrained to observe God's Law, and why they gave a solemn promise to be the people of God forever unless we understand that they were also accorded the authority, and the capacity, to defend themselves from perjury and the Church from devastation? Why, in other words, a Covenant with the people to be God's people if they may, and even must, allow themselves to be led by their kings to the worship of strange gods? Why an agreement that God is to be worshipped purely if the people, in the position of slaves, can contract no obligation? And, finally, if the people may not act to discharge their obligation as they promised, why then did God make a solemn Covenant with persons who have no right either to promise or perform? The truth, rather, is that, in making a Covenant with the people, God wished to give us clear-cut evidence that the people had the right, not only of making a Covenant, but also of performing it and of enforcing its performance. For if we agree that contracts made with slaves and servants are ridiculous and will not be noticed by the courts [in civil law], it would be impudent of us to attribute a compact of this sort to God. . . .

[Prophets appealed to the people, or rather the assembled estates of the people, to act against idolatrous kings. Failure of the people to act was punished by God. There are many examples of the punishment of the Israelites for their failure to correct a wicked king.]

It is, furthermore, the part of a good legislator not only to make sure that delinquencies are punished, but to prevent them from being committed, just as good physicians would rather prescribe diets to prevent disease than remedies for the symptoms. Hence, a religious people not only will restrain a prince in the act of doing violence to God's Law, but will, from the beginning, prevent gradual changes arising from his guilt or negligence, for the true worship of God may be slowly corrupted over extended periods of time. Moreover, they will not only refuse to tolerate crimes committed against God's majesty in public, but will constantly strive to remove all occasions for such crimes. We, thus, read that King Hezekiah, with Israel convened in public assembly, warned those who lived beyond the Jordan to smash the bronze serpent they had made and also the altar they had built for it.

It is, then, not only lawful for Israel to resist a king who overturns the Law and the Church of God, but if they do not do so, they are guilty of the same crime and are subject to the same penalty. Hence, if they are attacked with words, they will resist with words, but if with force, with force, and with stratagems, I say, as well as open warfare. For if deception is encountered, they will resort to licit deception of their own. If a war is just, it makes no difference whether one fights in the open or through ruses, as long as trickery is always distinguished carefully from treachery, which is never permissible.

But here an objection is to be anticipated. Do you really mean, it will be said, that the entire multitude, that many-headed monster, should go rushing into matters of this sort like a raging flood? Can order be expected from the mob? Or wisdom for settling affairs?

When we speak of the people collectively, we mean those who receive authority from the people, that is, the magistrates below the king who have been elected by the people or established in some other way. These take the place of the people assembled as a whole and are ephors to kings and associates in their rule. And we also mean the assembly of the Estates, which are nothing less than the epitome of a kingdom to which all public matters are referred. The seventy elders of the kingdom of Israel were magistrates of this sort. They were originally chosen from the tribes that went into Egypt, six from each, and, with the high priest presiding, they decided all important questions. And there were also the chiefs or heads of the individual tribes, the judges and officials of the several districts, *i.e.,* the captains of the thousands and captains of the hundreds, who presided over groups of families; and finally the nobles and the notables and so on. All of these composed the public council, the meetings of which are very often reported in terms like "the elders w   assembled at Raman" as in the election of Saul, or "all Is   ." or "all Judah," or "all Benjamin," etc., when it is unlik   at the entire multitude assembled.

In every properly const   ed kingdom, this is the character of the officers of the crown, the peers, the lords, the patricians, the notables, and others chosen by the several estates who, in various combinations, make up the membership of the ordinary or the extraordinary council—the parliament *(parlamentum),* diet, and other such assemblies, which have different names in different regions. The office of all of these is to see that no harm is suffered either by the commonwealth or by the Church. For although these officers are severally below the king, they are collectively above him. Just as an Ecumenical Council is above the Pope, as was rightly decided at the Councils of Basel and Constance, and just as the cathedral chapter is above the bishop; a corporation, above its representative *(actor);* a court above its president; and as generally one who receives authority from an aggregate is inferior to the aggregate even if superior to each individual member; so there can be no doubt that Israel, which chose and established its king as a kind of public representative *(actor),* was superior to Saul, who was established at Israel's initiative and for Israel's benefit, as we shall further show below. Since, therefore, good government depends on a degree of order that cannot be maintained in a large multitude, and since affairs of state often cannot be communicated publicly without danger to the common interest, everything that we have maintained was granted and entrusted to the people as a whole applies rather to the officers of the kingdom; and whatever we say is granted and entrusted to Israel refers to its princes and its elders, and this is indicated by the way they act. . . .

[The point is illustrated by the deposition and execution of Athaliah, who, as queen mother, had taken control of the government in violation of a fundamental law of Judah excluding women from the throne, and who had also governed tyrannically. Punishment was at the hand of Jehoiada, the high priest, who had rallied certain notables.]

She [Athaliah] was therefore justly punished—and by one who was acting in accordance with his office. For Jehoiada was not a private subject but the high priest, whose jurisdiction extended to civil matters also. Furthermore, he had all the princes of Judah and the Levites on his side and was himself related to the [infant] king. Although he did not summon the customary assembly at Mizpah, he was not criticized for this; nor was he criticized for planning and conspiring in secret. A conspiracy is good or bad as its aim is good or bad, and as those involved in it are good or not. The princes of Judah were, therefore, right in proceeding as they did and would have been wrong if they had acted otherwise. For just as a guardian must look to the welfare of his ward and is subject to legal action for neglect, so these officials must protect the safety of the people, which has put itself in their collective care and stewardship, and which has, in a sense, given them all of its own power of initiative.

Thus, as a whole people is permitted to oppose a tyrant, so also are the principal persons of the kingdom, who represent the body of the people, in the same manner that municipal officials may make contracts for the good of the entire corporation. And as the decisions of the majority of a corporation publicly arrived at are taken as the decisions of the entire body, so the action of the majority of princes and notables is taken to be that of all of them, and what all of them have done is regarded as an act of the people as a whole.

May a Part of the Kingdom Resist?

But here we face another question. Let us suppose that a king is aiming to abolish the Law of God and His Church, and that the people generally, or a clear majority, has consented, and that all the principal persons, or the greater part of them,

have failed to act against the tyrant. Now let us also suppose
that a very small part of the people, and just one of the principal persons and magistrates, wish to maintain and preserve
God's Law and worship God correctly. What may they do if
the king should try to force that part of the people to practice
idolatry or to keep them from true worship?

Now we are not speaking here of private individuals, who
are not to be regarded as the basic parts of a community any
more than planks, nails, and pegs are taken as the parts of a
ship; or stones, beams, and mortar as the parts of a house. We
are speaking rather of a province or a town, which is a part
of the kingdom in the same way the prow, deck, and rudder
are the parts of a ship, or the roof, walls, and foundation are
the parts of a house. And we are also speaking of the magistrate who is in charge of that province or town. . . .

[The revolt of Libnah against Jehoram, of the Maccabees
against Antiochus, and of Deborah against Jagin, the king of
the Canaanites, are cited as cases in which parts of Israel
repudiated a ruler in the name of religion.]

We have already said that the king took an oath to maintain
the Law of God as far he was able, and that Israel as a whole,
taken as a single entity, likewise gave its promise to observe
God's stipulations. We now say that each of the towns that form
part of the kingdom, and also the magistrates of each, have
individually and expressly sworn to do the same insofar as
they were directly affected. And this is a rule that all Christian
cities and communities have tacitly observed. . . .

[The Biblical citations that follow are designed to show that
the presence in the assembly of the whole people, of the towns
and communities, or the magistrates thereof, was taken as
implying the responsibility of each. The basic argument is the
same as in the following example.]

When an emperor is to be inaugurated in the German Empire, the electors and princes, lay and ecclesiastical, are present
either in person or through deputies; as are the prelates, counts,
and barons; and, finally, delegates from all the towns of the
Empire with special mandates to submit and bind themselves,
as well as those they represent, to the Emperor. Hence if some-

one who has recognized the Emperor should now drive him from office and seize his place, the princes and the barons must surely deny this usurper the aids and tributes owed the emperor, unless they would not only connive in his misfortune, but actually conspire with his adversaries, in violation of their faith. But if this be so, do not the people of Strasbourg or of Nuremberg have a perfect right to shut their gates against the outlaw and to keep him out? Indeed, were they not to do so, and were they to give no aid to their Emperor in his distress, could it possibly be said that they fulfilled the faith they pledged? Indeed, the rule [of civil law] is that anyone who does not protect his superior when he is able to do so is as guilty as the attacker. But if this is so (and it is surely plain enough), do not the people of Libnah and of Modin have the same right and duty if God, whom they know they are bound to obey above all, is deserted by the other estates *(ordines)* of the kingdom? What, then, shall we say is the proper course for a town that desires to worship God in purity if a Jehoram or Antiochus should appear, who would suppress worship of the true God and would raise himself above God, and if Israel should cooperate or look the other way? . . .

[The town should not only persist in its worship but, if threatened by the tyrant, should close its gates against him and resist. The towns are not, as some would argue, the king's property. They have individually joined in the covenant with God. Furthermore, it is not the town that rebels, but the king who provokes resistance by rebelling against God. The town will return to obedience as soon as the king desists from his disobedience. The town's action, in shutting its gates, is an act of self-defense that ceases when the threat has passed, and so the Maccabees recognized King Demetrius once he accorded them freedom of worship. In addition, the right of a subdivision to resist is even confirmed by the doctors of the Sorbonne, who legitimized many actions by French kings to protect the French Church against the Pope. The Sorbonnists argued that resistance to Boniface VIII (among others) was not schismatic, since the separation was not from the Church or from the Pope, but from Boniface, and the separation could continue without taint of schism until an honest Pope was named.]

Hence, we may say in summary that a people, acting through the authorities that have the power of the people in them, or through the greater part of these authorities, can and should use force against a prince who commands unholy action or prohibits holy ones. Also, all, or at least the leading citizens, of the several towns, acting under their chief magistrates, may rightfully drive out idolatry from their walls and foster true religion. Furthermore, since the Church is ever one, they may extend its confines, and if they do not do so when they have the power, they are guilty of treason against God.

May Private Persons Resist by Force of Arms?

It only remains to consider the case of private persons. In the first place, individuals in their private capacity are not bound by the Covenant between God and the people as a whole in which it promises to be God's people. For what is owed a corporation is not owed to any single individual, and the debts of a corporation are not owed by any single individual. In the second place, private individuals are not obligated [to resist] by any office. Each individual is bound to serve God in the vocation to which he is called. But private persons have no power, discharge no magistracy, and have no dominion [imperium] or right of punishment [ius gladii]. And since God did not give the sword to private persons, He does not require them to use it. To private persons it is said: "Put thy sword into its scabbard"; to magistrates, however: "You do not bear the sword in vain." The first are guilty if they draw the sword, the latter bear a heavy burden of guilt for neglect of duty if they do not draw it when the need arises.

What, it will be said, does God not covenant with private individuals as well as with the generality, and with humble men as well as magistrates? Why then circumcision? Why baptism? And why such frequent mention of the Covenant throughout the Bible? All of this is right, but very much beside the point. For just as the subjects of a good prince are all bound to obey no matter what their rank, and yet some, the magistrates, are specially obliged to make sure the rest obey, so all men are bound to serve God, but some, whose rank is higher, take on an even greater burden in that, if they neglect their duty, they are in some measure responsible for the guilt of all the others. Kings and magistrates, who have received the sword from the people as a whole, should make sure that the general body of the Church is rightly governed; private individuals, that they are members of the Church. The former must see that the Temple of God is not ruined or polluted and is safe against corruption from within and damage from without; the latter, that their own body, which is God's Temple, is not impure and is fit for the dwelling of God's Spirit. "Whosoever shall destroy God's Temple, which you are," says [St.] Paul, "him shall God destroy." For this reason, the authorities are armed with the visible sword. To private persons, only the sword of the spirit is commended. And this is the Word of God, with which [St.] Paul arms all Christians against the onslaught of the devil.

But what may private subjects do if the king would drive them to idolatry? If the leading men, who hold authority from the people as a whole, or else the local magistrates, should intervene, private persons should obey and follow and use all their energy and zeal as soldiers on the side of God to support these holy enterprises. And as one example among many, they may take the unhesitating obedience of the officers and soldiers to the princes of Judah, who, at Jehoiada's urging, saved the kingdom from the tyranny of Athaliah. But if the notables and magistrates go on doing honor to a maddened king or simply initiate no effort to resist him, private persons should follow the advice of Christ and go to another city. An example for them is the faithful of the ten tribes of Israel, who went to the kingdom of Judah, where the worship of the true God continued, after it had been suppressed in Israel by Jeroboam with the connivance of the other authorities. And if they cannot flee, they should rather give up life than God and rather be crucified themselves than again crucify Christ, as the Apostle says. . . .

[The resistance of Moses against Pharaoh, of Ehud against Eglon, and of Jehu against Jehoram were not, as they might perhaps appear, the deeds of private individuals. Since all of them were specially called by God, they possessed an authority

surpassing even that of magistrates. At least in principle, therefore, private persons may initiate resistance if they are specially
summoned for that purpose.]

But where God has not spoken with His own mouth or
through His prophets in extraordinary fashion, we must be
extremely circumspect and sober. Let any man who would
assume a responsibility like that, as though he felt the inspiration of God's Spirit, make sure that it is not his own arrogance
that swells within him, that he does not confuse himself with
God, that these great inspirations of his are not creations of
his own, and that he does not, therefore, conceive vanities and
beget lies. And let the people be sure that, in hastening to
enlist under the banners of Christ, they are not enrolling with
some Theudas of Galilee or Bar-Kochba—and bring evil on
themselves (which is what happened to the inhabitants of
Münster not so long ago in Germany). I do not say that the
same God who has sent us Pharaohs and Ahabs in this age
may not inspire liberators also, in some extraordinary way.
For His justice and His mercy are the same in any age. And
if we are given no evident external signs, we should at least
look for these internal signs through their effects—absence of
all ambition, genuine and earnest zeal, conscientiousness, and
finally, learning—which indicate a man who will not be led by
error to the service of false gods or be driven by the passions
of ambition to worship of himself rather than the true God.

May Force Be Used in the Cause of Religion?

But to remove all scruple we must answer those who believe
that the Church may not be defended by force or, more probably, would at least have it appear that this is their belief. . . .

[Old Testament examples of resort to arms in defense of
religion are advanced. The coming of Christ does not remove
the rights of magistrates. There have been, furthermore, many
wars by Christians to defend true religion.]

Thus, although the Church is not enlarged by arms, by arms
may it justly be defended. Nor are those who died in holy
wars any less martyrs than those who suffered on the cross.
Indeed, the path of the first would even seem to be the better

one. The merit of the latter is only not to have objected to the death that threatened them. The former knowingly, yet prudently, assumed the risk.

The Turks attempt to spread their doctrine by the force of arms. Whenever they subject a country, they introduce the unholy dogmas of Mohammed, relying upon force exclusively, for in his Koran Mohammed recommends the use of force so highly that he does not shrink from calling it the path to Heaven, although the Turks force no one to convert. But much worse, by far, are those enemies of Christ and true religion, and of the kings they have won over by their spells, who oppose the Gospel's light with flames, the Word of God with blows, and the sword of the Spirit with a battle line of steel, who use threats of torture to herd everyone they can to their unholy rites and are not ashamed to defend what they please to call the faith by faithlessness and to promote belief by endless treacheries.

Defense of true religion, on the contrary, is when pious magistrates and princes fence in and fortify the vine of Christ, where it exists or is to be implanted, against the depredations of wild boars; when they make sure that those converted to the true religion by the preaching of the Word are protected by their shields and guarded by their swords; and when, with wall, trench, and rampart, they fortify God's Temple built of living flesh against the violent onslaughts of the wicked, until it has reached its fullest height.

So much, then, to remove all qualms about our second question. We have shown that the people as a whole, or the officers of the kingdom whom the people have established, or the majority of these, or any one of them, very gravely sin against the Covenant with God if they do not use force against a king who corrupts God's Law or prevents its restoration, in order to confine him to his proper bounds. Residents of towns and provinces, which are the individual parts of a kingdom, are subject to the same penalty if they do not at least drive idolatry beyond their borders, when the ruler seeks to introduce it, and maintain true doctrine by whatever means they can, even if it means seceding temporarily at some point. Private persons, finally, have no excuse to obey sacrilegious commands. But beyond this they have no right whatsoever to take up arms on their own initiative unless they have clearly received an extraordinary calling. And all of this is evidenced by Holy Scripture.

The Third Question

May a prince who oppresses or devastates a common-wealth be resisted; and to what extent, by whom, in what fashion, and by what principle of law?

[What follows will be approved by proper kings and give offense to tyrants only.]

Kings Are Created by the People
. . . We have already shown that it is God who makes kings, gives kingdoms, and selects rulers. And now we say that it is the people that establishes kings, gives them kingdoms, and approves their selection by its vote. For God willed that every bit of authority held by kings should come from the people, after Him, so that kings would concentrate all their care, energy, and thought upon the people's interests. And kings are not to think that they are of a higher nature than the rest of men and rule as men rule over cattle. Born the same as all the rest of men, they are always to remember that they were raised up from below to their estates, upon all others' shoulders, as it were, so that thereafter the burdens of the commonwealth should fall, for the most part, upon theirs.

In ages past, when the people of Israel asked God for a king, God laid the foundation of their kingdom as we read in *Deuteronomy* 17:14–15. "When," says Moses, "you have come into the land that the Lord thy God has given you to possess, and when you have dwelt in it, you will say, 'Establish a king over me, like the kings of the other peoples living roundabout.'

Then will you establish the king whom thy God will choose for you from amongst thy brethren . . ." Here we see the King's selection attributed to God, his establishment to the people. And this, we read, is exactly how it happened in the actual event. The elders of Israel, who represented the people as a whole (for in this passage and throughout, the term "elders" also includes the captains of the thousands, the captains of the hundreds, the captains of the fifties, the captains of the tens, the judges and officers of all the tribes of Israel, as well as the princes and chiefs of each tribe more especially), met with Samuel at Ramah. And partly because they were tired of Samuel's sons, whose judgments were inequitable, and partly because they believed that their wars would be conducted better, they demanded a king of Samuel. Upon Samuel's request for counsel, God revealed that He had selected Saul to rule the people. And so Samuel anointed Saul. All of this, so far, bears on the selection of a king at the people's request, and it might have seemed sufficient for Samuel to present the people with the king whom God had chosen and to command them to obey. But in order that the king might know that he was established by the people, Samuel called an assembly at Mizpah, and there—as if the entire transaction had to be redone, as if, that is, the choice of Saul had not occurred—the lot was drawn. And it fell on someone from the tribe of Benjamin, and from the family of Matri, and within this family on Saul, whom God had chosen. Then only, with the acclamation of the people as a whole, was Saul considered king. But God also willed that royal status should not be attributed solely to lot. After Saul had given a token of his virtue by liberating Jabesh-Gilead from a siege by the Ammonites, he was confirmed as king in the presence of God by the whole people assembled at Gilgal, even though some of them dissented. We see, then, that the king whom God had chosen, who had been selected from all the rest by lot, became king by the votes of the people. . . .

[The role of the people in confirming David and Solomon is even clearer. The purpose of these elections, it is again pointed out, was less to give the people a choice than to remind rulers of their obligation. Election of kings, furthermore, was also practiced among the Medes and early Romans, and also by the Romans of the Empire until the custom was broken by the tyrant Nero.]

And since no one is born a king, and no one is a king by nature; and since a king cannot rule without a people, while a people can rule itself without a king, it is clear, beyond all doubt, that the people is prior to the king and that kings were originally established by the people. By adhering to the virtues of their forebears, the sons and relatives of kings sometimes seem to have rendered a kingdom hereditary, and in certain regions the right of free elections almost seems no longer to exist. And yet in all properly constituted kingdoms, the practice still remains inviolate. Children do not properly succeed to the fathers' thrones until they are established, as if *de novo,* by the people. They are not kings by birth, or by inheritance, but become kings only when they have received the office, together with the sceptre and the crown, from those who represent the people's majesty.

In Christian kingdoms now reputed to descend by succession, these traces of election are quite evident. The kings of France, Spain, England, and other countries are normally inaugurated by the estates of the realm—that is, by the peers, patricians, and magnates, who represent the people as a whole and who put the king into possession of the kingdom, as it were. In Germany, the emperors are chosen by the electors, and the king of Poland by the Wojewodowie, or palatines, since in both of these countries the right of election is preserved intact. Furthermore, the cities of a kingdom do not accord an incumbent regal honors until he has been properly inaugurated. And in ancient times the beginning of a reign was dated from the day of coronation, a practice followed very strictly in France. But so that we are not misled by recurrent series of direct successions in these kingdoms, it should be noted that the Estates have often preferred the uncle to the son, the younger brother to the elder—as in France Louis was preferred over his brother, Robert, Count of Evreux; and Henry, the king's brother, over Robert Capet, the surviving son of Henry's older brother. And in France the crown was also transferred from family to family by the authority of the people—from the Merovingians to the Carolingians and from these to the Capetians.

[Additional evidence of election in early French history is given.]

Thus, at the beginning all kings were elected. And even those who seem today to come to the throne by succession must first be inaugurated by the people. Furthermore, even if a people has customarily chosen its kings from a particular family because of its outstanding merits, that decision is not so unconditional that if the established line degenerates, the people may not select another. Indeed, even the nearest kin of the selected family are not born kings but are made such. At their birth they are considered not kings but rather candidates for kingship.

The People Is Greater than the King

Since kings, then, are created by the people, it seems to follow that the people as a whole is greater than the king. This is an implication of the term itself, since one who is created by another is considered his inferior. Potiphar set Joseph over his family; Nebuchadnezzar set Daniel over his provinces of Babylon; Darius created 180 governors to superintend his kingdom. Masters set up slaves; kings, ministers. And the people sets up a king as a kind of minister to the commonwealth. . . .

[Kings are made for the people, not the people for the king. The people are compared to the owner, the king to the pilot of a ship. The conquests of a king belong not to him but to the people. There can be no king without a people, but a people can exist without a king. A king is powerless if the people do not support him.]

The People as a Whole Is Represented by the Officers of the Kingdom Ordinarily and by the Assembly of the Estates Either Extraordinarily or Annually

Moreover, what we have said of the whole people also applies, as was shown in our second question, to those who lawfully represent the whole people of the kingdom or of a single region, and who are commonly called officers, not of the king, but of the kingdom. Officers of the king are created and removed at his discretion. When the king dies, their tenure ends, and they too are deemed to be in some sense dead. Officers of the kingdom, on the other hand, receive, or at least used to receive, their authority from the people in public council and cannot be removed unless that body consents. Hence, the former depend upon the king, the latter, on the kingdom; the former, on the supreme officer of the kingdom, that is, upon the king, the latter, upon the supreme dominion of the people on whom the king himself depends as well. The duty of the first is to look after the well-being of the king; the duty of the second is to look after the safety of the commonwealth. The charge of the first is that they should attend and wait upon the king like domestics on a master; of the second, that they should protect the people's rights and privileges and make sure that the king himself commits no crime against the people nor neglects his duty toward them. The former, finally, are ministers, servants, and domestics of the king established only to obey him; the latter, on the other hand, are like assistants *(assessores)* of the king in reaching legal judgment and are associates in the royal power, so that all of them are bound, just like the king, to look after the welfare of the commonwealth. The king is like a president among them who possesses only primacy of place. For as the entire people is above the king, so these officers, although below the king as individuals, are above him when taken as a body. . . .

Among very early kings, this limitation of power is evident enough. Ephron, king of the Hittites, did not venture to grant Abraham the right of burial without consulting the people; and Hemor, the Hevite king of Sichem, did not conclude an alliance with Jacob on his own, since matters of importance were by custom referred to the people. Such consultation was easily accomplished in ancient times when kingdoms were confined to a single city. But when kings began to extend their territory and the whole people could not be assembled in one place without confusion, officers of the kingdom were established to guard the people's rights on an ordinary basis but with the proviso that, should the need arise, either the whole people, or else a kind of epitome of the whole people, would be convened in

extraordinary assembly. This was the arrangement in the kingdom of Israel, whose constitution, as all political thinkers have
agreed, was the best. The king had his cupbearers, butlers,
chamberlains, and stewards or overseers, who looked after the
royal family. The kingdom had, as its officers, the seventy-one
elders and the chiefs elected from the several tribes, who took
care of the commonwealth in peace and war, and finally, the
magistrates of the municipalities, who looked after the affairs
of the several cities, as did the former of the kingdom as a
whole. When matters of very great importance had to be deliberated, these municipal officers were convened, and no high
affair of state could be decided if they were not consulted. Thus,
David convened them when he wanted to invest Solomon with
the kingdom, when he wished to have the political arrangements that he had restored examined and approved; and also
when the Ark was to be moved, and so on. For since these
officers represent the entire people, the entire people is said
to be assembled when they convene. . . .

[Further examples from the Old Testament are given, dealing mainly with the great powers of the Sanhedrin (Council of
Seventy-one) after the kingdom was divided. A number of
other kingdoms are then cited in which officers were created
to check the king: Persia, Sparta, Egypt, early Rome, the Roman
Empire, the German Empire, Poland. The deviant examples
of Turkey and Muscovy are set aside as barbaric aberrations
from the norm. All other states of modern times exhibit checks
on royal power. If these have decayed through negligence, it
is the duty of the principal officers of the kingdom to restore
them to their original vigor insofar as they are able.]

What shall we say, then, of kingdoms said to pass by succession? Exactly the same. The kingdom of France, not long
ago preferred to all the rest for the excellence of its laws and
institutions, has institutions of this sort that go back to its
earliest times. If incumbents in royal office do not discharge
their duties fully, they are constrained to do so nonetheless.
The king has a high steward of his own, his chamberlains, his
masters of the hunt, shield-bearers, cupbearers, and the like,
whose offices once depended so completely on the person of

the king that when he died those who were his servants seemed to have died as well. Even now, after mourning for a king is over, the grand steward, by formal declaration, dismisses the royal household and orders each member to make his own arrangements for the future. At the same time the French kingdom has its own officers: the mayor of the palace, later called the "constable"; the marshals; the admirals; the chancellor, or great secretary; the treasurers; as well as others, all of whom, at one time, could be created only in a public council of the Three Estates of the clergy, nobility, and people. The present procedure, which goes back to the time when the Parlement of Paris ceased to be ambulatory, is that officers of the kingdom are not confirmed in their positions until they have been accepted and approved by the Senate [Parlement] in Paris, nor can they be deprived of office without its authorization and consent. All of these officials, furthermore, swear allegiance to the kingdom, that is, the people, first, and only then to the king as its guardian—which is clear from the wording of their oaths. When the king presents the chancellor with the seal, the chancellor accepts it to protect and to defend the commonwealth (as is apparent from the words the king pronounces).

The kingdom of France also has its peers and associates of the king or, if one prefers, its patricians or fathers of the commonwealth, one named from each province of the kingdom. At his coronation the king takes an oath to them as though they were the kingdom as a whole, which shows they are the king's superiors. They, on the other hand, swear to protect, not the king, but his crown; to advise the commonwealth and the prince on the business of the commonwealth; and to lend assistance in peace and war—as is plainly stated in the formula of their office. They are thus the same as the peers of court, in Lombard law,* who not only sat with the lord of a fief when sentences were passed, but often took cognizance of disputes between the lord and his vassals. This patriciate of France, it can be shown, often adjudicated between the king and his

---

*A reference to the *Libri feudorum*, or *Books of Feudal Law*, included in the medieval edition of the *Corpus juris*. The *Libri feudorum* were based on Lombard customs.

subjects. And when Charles VI tried to sentence the Duke of Brittany, they intervened and objected that adjudications of this sort belonged not to the king but to the peers, whose authority could not be set aside.

Hence, even today, the Parlement of Paris, which is called the "court of peers" or "of patricians," is judge between the king and the people, and especially between the king and particular individuals, for it is supposed to give justice to the individual if the king should seek to act against him in contravention of the law. Furthermore, if the king passes any edict or decision in his private council, or if a war is to be declared or peace is to be made, as under Charles V not long ago, the authorization of the Senate must be asked. In fact, everything relating to the commonwealth has to be entered in the record of its acts, since nothing is considered ratified until approval has been given by the Senate. And to protect the Senators from intimidation by the king, there was a time when no one could be coopted to its ranks unless he had been nominated by the Senate, and no one could be deprived of office without its authorization and for a cause prescribed by law.

Finally, unless letters of the king are also signed by a secretary of the kingdom and unless his decrees are countersigned by the chancellor (who has the power to annul them [*cancellandi*]), they are invalid. And there are dukes, marquisses, counts, viscounts, barons, and chatelains; and also, in the towns, elders, vicars, consuls, syndics, *échevins,* and so on, who are established to protect the people within their jurisdiction. And although some of these offices are now hereditary, they were all conferred by the several towns and districts.

So much, then, for ordinary checks. Beyond these, there is the Assembly of the Three Estates, which was at one time summoned every year, and although it has met less regularly since, it is always convened in dire times at least. All the districts and towns of any importance sent deputies to this assembly; and commoners *(plebeii),* nobles, and ecclesiastics there met together publicly and decided all matters of importance to the commonwealth. The authority of this assembly, moreover, was unquestioned. Whether it concluded peace, made war, named a regent, or imposed a tax, anything it decreed was considered binding and inviolable. By its authority, kings were sent off to monasteries for extravagance, neglect, or tyranny; and an entire line might be deprived of succession to the throne by the same authority that called it to the kingship in the first place. Thus kings who had been created by consent were, by its withdrawal, driven out. And children who enjoyed an almost hereditary claim through imitation of their fathers' virtue were disinherited as unworthy or unsuitable if their character had degenerated or was disagreeable. It is, therefore, clear enough that [hereditary] succession was tolerated only insofar as it was a convenient remedy for rebellions, secessions, interregna, and other dangers of election. But where succession threatened even greater dangers, where the kingdom was in jeopardy of tyranny or a tyrant had usurped the throne, a lawful assembly of the people had unquestioned authority to expel a tyrannical or incompetent king, and to install a good king in his place, albeit very often from the old king's male relations on his father's side. The French took this practice over from the Gauls, as is clearly indicated in Caesar Bk. 5, where Ambiorix, king of the Eburones, avows that the powers of the kings of Gaul were such that the people lawfully assembled had no less authority over the king than the king over the people. And this is also documented by the example of Vercingetorix, who justified his plans to the assembled people.

In the kingdoms of Spain, and especially in Aragon, Valencia, and Catalonia, it is very much the same. In Aragon, the *Justicia,* as he is called, is the highest authority in the kingdom. The magnates, who represent the people, proudly address the king, at his coronation and every third year thereafter, in the following terms: "We are as strong as you; and above us both there is someone (the *Justicia* of Aragon is understood) who has more authority than you." Furthermore, there is no country in the world where a tax can be imposed without the authorization of some assembly like this. In England and Scotland, sovereignty *(summa rerum)* resides in the Parliament, which is normally convoked each year. By Parliament they mean the assembly of the estates of the realm in which bishops, counts, barons, and deputies from the towns and districts deliberate on the condition of the commonwealth and make decisions by their joint consent. And so inviolable is its authority that a king who abrogates what it has once decided is considered guilty of a crime. Moreover, all officers of the kingdom, including those who sit in the council of the king or queen, normally receive their insignia from this assembly.

Finally, it is clear, from written history or living memory, that the other Christian kingdoms—Hungary, Bohemia, Denmark, Sweden, and the rest—also have officials of the kingdom who are associates in the royal power and who have, on various occasions, even made use of that authority even to depose the king himself. Nor is it true to say that in this we show less esteem for royal power or suppose the dignity of kings to be diminished. We do not hold God less powerful because He cannot sin, or believe His authority restricted because He cannot wantonly destroy. Hence a king, who can sin, is not demeaned if he is sustained through others' help and, through others' prudence, enjoys long possession of a kingdom that he might otherwise lose through his own neglect and faults. . . .

Can the Rights of the People Be Lost by Prescription?

But you will perhaps object and say, You speak of peers, notables, and officials of the crown, while I see nothing but fading names and archaic costumes like the ones they wear in tragedies. I see scarcely any remnant of ancient authority and liberty. Look where you will, and you may find any number of officers assiduously flattering kings and deceiving peoples but hardly one who feels pity for a people in oppression or makes the slightest gesture to relieve their misery. And should one try or even think of trying, he is called a rebel and a traitor, is driven into exile, and must devote all his efforts to his own survival.

This is hard to answer, for such, indeed, is our condition. The arrogance of kings, and the collusion or neglect of notables, has been the rule so long that license, so ordinary among kings of our day, seems to be lawful by prescription. The people seem to have ceded their authority, or else to have lost it through disuse, for it often happens that the concern of all is the concern of none and that everyone's responsibility is assumed by no one. Nevertheless, prescription does not run against the people, and no collusion can affect their rights.

If, as is commonly said, prescription does not run against the royal treasury, then it runs even less against the people, for the people is greater than the king, and it is only for their benefit that the king's fisc has special privilege. And how else could it be, if the prince is but the treasury's administrator, while the people are its true proprietor, as will be shown below? Moreover, is it not also an accepted principle that liberty can never be prescribed by violence or by servitude, however long? And if you should object that kings were created by the people of 500 years ago and not by that which now exists, the answer is that although kings die, a people, like any corporate body, never dies. . . .

[The people, like a river, is perpetually renewed. In addition, each successive king receives the kingdom anew from the people and does not merely inherit from his father, who, in any case, could not transfer to his heir more rights than he possessed himself. Long connivance of magistrates casts doubts on the honor of these magistrates, not on the rights of the people. If magistrates have ceded any portion of the people's rights, the concession was in violation of their oath and so is invalid.]

The people, you may say, must take responsibility for having elected persons of this sort. But these officers are very much like patrons who are established to protect the public welfare and the people's liberty and safety. And just as courts of law will not decide against a client whose patron [attorney] has conspired with his adversary and has thus betrayed his cause, so no conspiracy by so-called "magistrates" for the injury or destruction of the people can effect subtraction from its rights. It is the patron, rather, who incurs a penalty for perjury. The client, on the other hand, is allowed by [civil] law to select a new patron to pursue his rights afresh and to proceed from his original position. . . .

The Reason for Creating Kings

Kings, then, are established by the people. And to keep them to their duty, they are given associates, as it were, who, though below the king as individuals, are together his superior. We may now ask, therefore, why kings were established in the first place and for what essential purpose. For to prove that a thing is just and good is to show that it attains the goal for which it was established. . . .

[Men created kings for their own advantage, not the kings.' They would not have surrendered their natural liberty, which they prize like any other animal, had they not anticipated great advantages. The foremost of these is the guarantee of justice by the king. The theme of the king as justice embodied is then embroidered with a number of traditional analogies and maxims.]

. . . [W]hen peoples began to feel the need for equal laws, they were prepared to accept them from a just and honorable individual. But men like that are scarce, and the outcome was often very different. In most cases, the only semblance of law was the discretionary judgment of the king, which spoke differently to different persons. This was the point at which learned men, together with the other magistrates, invented laws, which were to be the same for all. Henceforth the first obligation of a king was to be the guardian, minister, and protector of the laws. Kings, of course, could draw upon natural equity to supplement the law from time to time, since all eventualities could not be anticipated. But to prevent kings from doing violence to the law, notables were now appointed by the people to serve as associates to the king, and of these we have already spoken.

Let kings obey the law, then, and acknowledge law to be their queen. "I command as I will. Reason is anything I wish" is how Juvenal describes not the strength, but the weakness of a woman, and it should be taken as a form of madness. And let kings not feel that subjection to the law diminishes their dignity as rulers. Law is like an instrument, divinely given, through which human societies are ordered for the best and directed to a blessed end. A king who finds obedience to the law demeaning is therefore as ridiculous as a surveyor who considers the rule and compass and other instruments of skilled geometers to be disgraceful and absurd, or a captain who takes fancy as his guide and prefers to zigzag off in all directions rather than steer by the mariner's compass.

[Law is the soul of a good king. Law is reason freed of passion. Men may be corrupt; the law, never. To obey a king without the law or against the law is the same as to be subject to a beast. Absolute power is virtual tyranny, since no human being can exercise it properly. Indeed, no sensible man would want to have it.]

Kings Receive the Law from the People

. . . [I]n all properly constituted kingdoms, the king receives laws from the people, which laws he is obligated to protect and observe. If he violates or evades them, he is judged unjust. . . .

[Biblical, classical, and modern examples show that kings swear to uphold the laws at their coronation. Thus, they receive laws from the people together with their crown.]

May Kings Make New Laws?

Should kings, then, not even be permitted to repeal laws and make additions? The duty of a king is not only to stop violations of the law, but also to prevent evasion. He should, therefore, see that the law is free of omissions and redundancies; and that it does not grow obsolete and fade into oblivion, forgotten and unnoticed. If he sees something that ought to be repealed, replaced, or modified, he should convoke the people, or the notables of the people, either in ordinary or extraordinary assembly, advise them of the need, and request the legislation he proposes. But he may not enact anything as law until the assembly has deliberated and approved it. Once he has enacted it, moreover, it is too late for him to change his mind, for he is now obliged to keep it. Examples are more powerful than words, and the maker of a law should be its keeper. It is futile and even, in a sense, unjust for a prince to demand that his subjects should obey laws that he, their custodian, ignores. The quality by which a king is most properly distinguished from his subjects is his equity or justice, not [his] impunity. . . .

[The example of Augustus and a saying of Solon's are cited in illustration.]

Thus, if the Emperor of Germany thinks a law is needed, he proposes it first to the assembly, and if it is approved, the princes, barons, and deputies of the towns affix their signatures, at which point it is considered law. The Emperor also swears that he will keep the laws that have been passed and will not make new ones without general consent. There is a law in the kingdom of Poland that new ordinances may not be made without public consent, which must be given in the assembly and no place else. In France, where royal authority is commonly thought to be extremely great, laws used to be passed in the Assembly of the Three Estates or in the itinerant royal council. Now that the Parlement is stationary, royal edicts are invalid until that Senate gives them its approval. On the other hand, if the law is incomplete, decrees of the Senate, that is, of the Parlement of Paris, generally obtain the force of law. In the kingdoms of England, Spain, Hungary, and so on, the procedure of olden times is still in force. . . .

[The king has no discretionary power of life and death over subjects.

The power of kings to pardon on equitable grounds is reluctantly conceded. But it must be exercised only to prevent manifest injustice, and then only on advice. In France the power to pardon is subject to control by the chancellor and the judges.

A prudent king will look upon his people more as brethren than subjects, since the people's affection is his main resource.]

Does the King Own Everything?

The king, then, has no arbitrary power over life. We must now inquire whether he does not, at least, have title to all property. And we shall begin the discussion with the property of private individuals.

Nowadays the courts of princes are full of people who say that the king owns everything, that what he takes from his subjects is so far from theft that anything he leaves them is a temporary gift of usufruct. This idea has so captivated the minds of certain princes that they do not shrink from saying that their poor subjects are like teams of oxen. When they plough, when they grind, they are always ploughing and grinding for their prince. And although this is a clear violation of the law, it is surely the rule that princes follow.

We should always remember that kings were created for the people's benefit, that rulers are called "kings" when they promote the people's interest and are called "tyrants," as Aristotle says, when they seek only to promote their own. Since each man loves his own and many men even covet the property of others, what kind of ruler were they most likely to have sought —a prince on whom to bestow all they had acquired by their labor, or one who would assume responsibility for guaranteeing the property of each, of the poor man no less than of the rich; a prince who would look on everything as his, or one who would render to each his own; a prince who would squander the fruits of other people's labor like a drone, or one who would keep their honey safe; a prince, finally, who would invade their properties himself, or one who would try to keep out invaders from abroad? What difference does it make to me, the husbandman will say, whether my property is stolen by a foreign invader or the king? In either case I die of hunger. What difference to me whether a foreigner or fellow citizen ransacks my barn, carries off my stores, or levels my house? In either case I am hungry, ruined, and exposed. What difference to me whether the soldiers who seize me are barbarians or Romans; either way I die. Why, he will ask, should I call the foreigner barbaric if my countrymen are such as you? And why should anyone be called a tyrant when you enjoy the name of king? If parricide is worse than homicide, are not the crimes of kings proportionately worse than those of enemies?

If, therefore, men did not surrender all their property to kings when they created them, but entrusted them with its protection, what title, other than the law of pirates, can justify the claim of kings to everything? The Pharaohs of Egypt were not masters in their own right over the private property of individuals. They took this title only after they purchased these properties for corn, and even so the validity of the sales is doubtful and not beyond dispute. Ahab, king of Israel, could not force Naboth to sell his vineyard to him. The Roman emperors, although their vast authority is always cited, could claim no greater right. And today there is not a single kingdom in which even the humblest of private persons may not sue the king before his judges; and should the king lose, as very often happens, he is obligated to obey the judgment as much as private persons. Nor may it be objected that certain servants of the emperors have written that the king holds everything by civil law, that everything is somehow Caesar's. The same writers interpret this to mean that the king has dominion only over everything in general, private individuals, dominion over all the several parts; that Caesar possesses everything in his political capacity, individuals, in their capacity as private owners. It is a rule well-established among jurists that a claim to a ship or to a house is not necessarily a claim to the planks or to the stones. Similarly, the king of Germany, or France, or England, may claim the kingdom as a whole and vindicate that claim in court, and yet he may not, without notorious injustice, exclude any person from his private property on the ground that he who possesses everything collectively ought to be and is, by law, the owner of all things taken severally.

Is the King the Owner of the Kingdom?

Does the king, then, have private property in the royal, or public, patrimony? We must treat this topic in even more detail. The first thing to note is that the patrimony of the royal treasury is one thing, the patrimony of the prince, another. In other words, I say that the possessions of the emperor, of the king, or of the prince are completely distinct from the possessions of Antoninus, of Henry, or of Philip. The king receives the former from the people, the latter from his family. This distinction is encountered frequently in civil law, which carefully differentiates the public from the princely patrimony, the treasury of Caesar from the public treasury, the procurators of Caesar's treasury from the procurators of the emperor's, the distributors of public funds from the distributors of Caesar's revenue, the officials of the public treasury from the officers of Caesar's private wealth. This distinction is so sharp that the emperor who, as emperor, is preferred to private persons as a creditor in mortgage actions, may, as Antoninus, have lower priority than other claimants. Similarly, in the German Empire the goods of Maximilian of Austria are distinct from those of Emperor Maximilian, and the treasurers of the empire are separate from his own. Indeed, this even extends to the magnates of the empire. The legal status of their family inheritances differs from that of the possessions connected with their office as electors. And even with the Turks, the patrimony, or estates, of Selim are distinguished from the treasury estates, the first being designated for the prince's table, the second only to sustain the empire.

There are also kingdoms like France, England, and others where the king has no personal inheritance at all, but only the public patrimony granted by the people, so that the distinction is irrelevant. Nevertheless, where private possessions of the king exist, he is clearly the proprietor and by civil law may sell or spend them at his own discretion like any other private person. But it is equally certain that the king is in no sense the proprietor of the royal patrimony, or the public treasury, which is commonly known as the domain. . . .

How could it be otherwise? If someone has made you shepherd of his flocks, did he empower you to slay, shear, sell, and deliver it at his own pleasure? And if the people made you duke or magistrate of a town or district, did it empower you to alienate, sell, or cede it? And since the population of a region that is alienated are ceded with it, did they then empower you to trade, prostitute, and enslave them? Let me ask, furthermore, whether royal status is a possession or an office *(functio)*. If it is an office, what does it have in common with a property? If it is a possession, then is it not at least a form of possession whereby the people, who conferred it, retain the proprietary right? Finally, if the public patrimony or domain is truly called the "dowry of the commonwealth," and if the dissolution or waste of that dowry means that the commonwealth, the kingdom, and at last the king himself are lost, is there any legal principle imaginable that could make alienation of that dowry permissible?

[Several examples are given of negligent or insane kings, who gave away the domain and were therefore unable to protect their subjects. Since it is for the protection of the people that kings were instituted, it follows, as a rule of natural law, that diminution or waste of the public domain is unlawful and tyrannical.]

When kings were created, it was necessary, of course, to provide them with resources. This was in part to keep them as befits a king, but in part also, and much more important, to provide for royal expenses. Both honesty as well as utility required this. Royal expenses included the establishment throughout the realm of provincial judges, who would not take gifts and would not prostitute the law for money; and also the maintenance of officers to enforce court decrees where necessary, and to keep roads and commerce safe, and so on. When war seemed imminent, it was also necessary to garrison towns against the enemy, to erect walls, and to build arsenals. Furthermore, it is well known that peace cannot be guaranteed without preparedness for war, war cannot be sustained without soldiers, nor soldiers without pay, nor pay without taxes. And as the domain was instituted to defray the costs of peace, so was taxation (which jurists call the "canon"*), to defray the costs of war, although in cases of unusual danger extraordinary imposts could be laid. . . .

[Taxes are legitimate only when they are spent for the immediate purposes of war.

Since war is a public undertaking, the spoils of war belong to the people, not the king.

On similar reasoning, the material advantages accruing from a royal marriage belong to the public. Presumably, the king would not have succeeded as a suitor if it had not been for his public status.

To guarantee that taxes will be used for public purposes,

---

*In late classical Latin *canon*, in one of its meanings, referred to certain imperial taxes. In later medieval Latin, it referred to guns as well.

the kings of Europe do not impose taxes without the authorization of the estates.]

In former times the kings of France passed all measures of taxation in the Assembly of the Three Estates. Hence the law of Philip of Valois that no contributions would be levied except in dire emergencies and with the consent of the estates. And these contributions used to be kept in strongboxes in the several dioceses and entrusted for safekeeping to selectmen (who are called, indeed, "*élus*") to provide pay for soldiers recruited in the area. This used to be the practice in other countries also, as in Belgium, for example. And even today, at the very minimum, measures of taxation are not considered valid unless the senate has consented. And there are some provinces which, by separate agreement, cannot be bound except by the consent of their estates. These include Languedoc, Brittany, Provence, Dauphiné, and others, as well as almost all the provinces of Belgium. Everywhere, therefore, limits are placed upon the treasury so that it will not become a swollen spleen, which deprives the other members of their nourishment and devours everything itself. . . .

[Kings who collect taxes for their private purposes are tyrants. The administration of finances may be taken from the hands of a spendthrift king and reordered.

Numerous examples show that the king has no right to alienate royal domain.]

In the case of France, on which I shall dwell longer since it is illustrative of all the rest, the vigor of this principle has never ceased. The law prohibiting alienation of the domain is the oldest in the kingdom. Born together with the kingdom, as it were, it has been renewed as recently as 1566, even though it has been poorly kept. Two cases of alienation are exempted from the rule. One is the assignment of an appanage (or stipend) to the children or brothers of the king—but on condition that the right of subinfeudation is fully reserved. The other is a cession of territory dictated by necessity of war—but only on condition that the treaty provides for its redemption. In olden days, neither was considered valid unless it was ordained by the Assembly of the Estates. And now that the Parlement has become a stationary body, the Parlement, or Senate, at Paris must approve, as also the Chamber of Accounts, and even the treasurer-generals according to edicts of Charles VI and Charles IX. And so deeply rooted is this principle that the early kings of France had to ask consent from the notables even to endow a church, although that was a kind of enterprise much favored in those days.

When the king of France is crowned at Rheims, he swears to observe this law [on the domain]. And if he violates it, his gift is so utterly invalid that he might just as well make a present of the Turkish or the Persian Empire. Hence the ordinances of Philip VI, Jean II, Charles V, Charles VI, and Charles VIII invalidating all alienations granted by their predecessors. Hence also the revocation by the estates assembled at Tours, in the presence of Charles VIII, of many alienations granted by his father, Louis XI, and the dispossession of the heirs of Louis XI's favorite, Tancred of Chastel, of the villages that Louis had given Tancred on his own authority. . . .

So much then of the public domain. And to make it even clearer that the kingdom is greater than the king, it should be noted that the ruler, having received his majesty from the people, may not diminish it on his own authority. He may not declare any subject outside of his protection, nor may he cede the right of majesty over any part of the kingdom whatsoever. . . . But, omitting many further examples on this point, I ask by what right a king may give away or sell the kingdom or any part of it, since it consists of people not of walls. Free persons cannot be objects of exchange since even freedmen cannot be compelled by a patron to establish their domicile any place other than where they please. This all the more obviously applies to subjects in that they are not servants but brethren of the king. And not only are they, as individuals, the brethren of the king, but, taken collectively, they are properly the owners of the kingdom.

Is the King the Usufructuary of the Kingdom?

If the king is not, then, proprietor of the kingdom, may he not at least be called the usufructuary of its domain? But he is not a usufructuary either. A usufructuary may mortgage what he holds, and we have said that the king may not mortgage the patrimony of the fisc. A usufructuary may give away his income as he pleases. Excessive gifts by the king, however, are considered void; unnecessary expenditures are rescinded; superfluities are cut. Anything diverted to other than public use is considered stolen. And the king is bound by the *lex Cincia** no less than any private Roman citizen. In France, particularly, gifts by the king are not valid without the consent of the Chamber of Accounts. Hence the annotation of this ordinary Chamber during the reigns of spendthrift kings: *"Trop donné, soit repeté"* ("This gift was excessive, and should be recovered"). The Chamber solemnly swears that, no matter what commands it receives from the king, it will approve nothing detrimental to the kingdom and the commonwealth, even though it is not always conscientious in enforcing this. The law, finally, is not concerned with how a usufructuary uses and enjoys his income. But it does prescribe the way in which a king must use his revenues. Thus, the early kings of France were obliged to divide the yield of the domain into four parts. One was to support the ministers of the Church and to help the poor; another was for the prince's table; a third was to pay his domestic servants; and the last was for the upkeep of castles, bridges, and royal dwellings. We also learn from historians that when the Assembly of the Three Estates was convened at Paris around 1412, there was a great commotion because Charles VI had altered this procedure to serve his own and his associates' cupidity and had increased the French budget, which hitherto had not exceed 94,000 francs, to 540,000 despite the impoverished condition of the commonwealth.

And as income from the domain was allocated in the manner just described, authorized subsidies were set aside for war, while levies, or tailles, were used only for the pay of soldiers.

The rulers of other kingdoms do not have more authority, and in many they have even less, as, for example, in the Ger-

---

*The *lex Cincia* is a Roman law dating from 204 B.C. that places a limit on the size of gifts by private persons. If a gift exceeded the limit, its donor could, if he chose, recover the excess.

man Empire and in Poland. But we preferred to illustrate the rule with French institutions so that bold injustice will not be mistaken for magnitude of legal right. . . .

[The principle that the rights of the people may not be prescribed is used to argue that violations of the rule against alienation, of which there have been many, are abuses rather than precedents. It is also asserted that even if the rule were not expressly written, it would follow from a law of nature, namely, that kings are established for the public interest.]

In conclusion, then, we have established that kings are neither owners nor usufructuaries of the royal patrimony, but are only its administrators. And this being so, they are even less able to claim the private property of individuals as their own, or the public property owned by the individual municipalities.

But before we continue, one source of doubt should be removed. After the people of Israel had requested a king, God said to Samuel, "Heed the people's voice, but first explain to them the kind of justice they will receive from the king who will rule over them." Then Samuel told them that the king would seize their fields, their vineyards, and their olive orchards and give them to his servants; that he would take their private possessions for himself; and would at last reduce them to slavery. It is indeed remarkable that this one passage should be so dear to sycophants who mock at all the rest of Scripture! God wishes here to show the people of Israel their own foolishness. They once had God within their midst to give them upright and religious men as judges and generals. Yet they preferred the uncertain rule of a mere human, who is prone to change with every passing hour, to the rule of the immortal God. He therefore showed them how slippery is the place on which a king is perched, how he may slide into violence very easily, how a kingship changes into tyranny, how the king whom he would give them would turn his sword against them, use his power for perverted ends, and put justice in the hands of force, and how the risk of evil they would so lightly take upon themselves would be experienced directly some day when redress was no longer available. It is, therefore, not the rights of kings that are described in the foregoing passage, but the right that kings so often arrogate; not what kings are permitted by their office, but what most of them usurp from wickedness. . . .

[The point is elaborated with further citations. It is argued that, in emphasizing the corruptibility of one man, Samuel was suggesting that the people of Israel should put a bridle on their kings, which, in fact, they did.]

The Covenant, or Compact,* Between the King and the People.

We have already said that the creation of a king involved a double compact. The first, between God, the king, and the people, has been discussed above. The second, between the king and the people, we shall now take up.

When Saul is made king, he accepts a *lex regia*** as the condition of his rule. David at Hebron, in the presence of God—with God, that is, as witness—enters into a covenant with all the elders of Israel, who represented the people as a whole. Joash, too, covenanted with the people of the land in the House of the Lord, with the high priest Jehoiada presiding. We are told, indeed, that a "testimony" was imposed on him, and many interpreters take this to mean the Word of God which, in many passages, is called the "testimony." And Josiah also promises that he will observe the precepts, testimonies, and commandments included in the Book of the Covenant, and he is thus referring to the precepts of religion and justice.

In all the relevant passages, the compact is said to be made with the whole people, or the entire multitude, or all the elders, or all the men of Judah—so that we may understand, even if it were not expressly stated, that not only did the chiefs of the tribes attend, but also the lesser military chiefs and lower magistrates acting in the name of the towns, each of which covenanted of its own right with the king.

This compact created the king. For the people made the king,

*Foedus sive pactum. Here and throughout *foedus* and *pactum* are used as equivalent. *Foedus* is the favored term where the agreement with God is mentioned. I have most often translated it as "covenant."

**Here used in a general sense as the "fundamental law of a kingdom." Cf. above, note on p. 12.

not the king the people. Therefore, there is no doubt that the people was the stipulator and the king the promiser. And the position of the stipulator is considered stronger under civil law. The people asked, by way of stipulation, whether the king would rule justly and according to the law. He then promised to do so. And the people, finally, replied that they would faithfully obey, as long as his commands were just. Hence, the promise of the king was absolute, that of the people was conditional; and if he does not perform, the people, by the same principle of civil law, are released from any obligation.

By the first covenant, or compact, religious piety becomes an obligation; by the second, justice. In the first the king promises to obey God religiously, in the second, to rule the people justly; in the former, to maintain God's glory, in the latter, to preserve the people's welfare. The condition in the first is: "If you will observe My Law"; the condition in the second is: "If you will render each his own." If the king does not perform the conditions of the first, God is properly the avenger, while the whole people may lawfully punish non-performance of the second.

In all legitimate governments a compact is always to be found. After sacrifices were performed, the Persians made the following covenant with Cyrus: "Do you, Cyrus, promise to support your country with all your might against anyone who wars against the Persians or violates their laws?" After he responds, they said, "We Persians will support you if anyone refuses to obey, as long as your commands are for the defense of the country." Xenophon calls this agreement a *"symmachia,"* that is, a mutual agreement *(confoederationem),* just as Isocrates calls his oration on the duty of subjects toward a prince *Symmachion Logon.* The covenant between the kings of Sparta and the ephors was renewed each month, even though the kings were always from the line of the Hercules. The kings swore that they would rule according to the law; the ephors, that they would maintain the kings in possession of their kingdom if they kept their promise. In the Roman kingdom, similarly, Romulus made a compact with the Senate and the people that the people would make the laws and he would enforce them, that the people would declare wars and he would conduct them. And even though most Roman emperors came to power more by force and fraud than by lawful procedure, and even though they arrogated every species of power in the name of the *lex regia,** as it is called, it is sufficiently clear from the fragments of that law found in books and in Roman inscriptions that the power which it granted was to protect and administer the commonwealth, not to disrupt and oppress it tyrannically. The good emperors, indeed, avowed that they were bound by law. They accepted their office from the Senate, referred the most important questions to it, and considered it improper to make any great decision until the Senate was consulted.

And if we look at modern kingdoms, we find none deemed worthy of the name in which this kind of compact between the prince and his subjects is not a regular procedure. In the German Empire, not so long ago, the King of the Romans,** who was about to be crowned emperor, used to pledge fealty and homage to the Empire, like a vassal to his lord when the vassal is invested with a fief. And although the form of the oath has been somewhat altered by the Popes, the substance still remains the same. We know, for example, that Charles V of Austria, and his successors, were elected emperors under definite rules and conditions, the sum of which is as follows: that the emperor would maintain established law, that he would not make new ones without consulting the electors, and that he would neither alienate nor mortgage any of the domain belonging to the Empire—all of which articles are expressly enumerated by historians. Further, when an emperor is crowned at Aachen, the Archbishop of Cologne, speaking first as the stipulator, asks, "Will you defend the Church, do justice, and preserve the Empire? And will you make sure that orphans and all others who deserve our pity are protected?" And he is not anointed and does not receive the sword as defender of the Empire or any of the other imperial insignia until he has taken that oath. It is therefore clear enough that the emperor is obligated absolutely, the princes of the Empire, but conditionally.

*See above, note on p. 12.

**The title of the emperor-elect before his coronation.

In the kingdom of Poland the practice is similar, as none will doubt who is familiar with the ritual very recently performed at the election and coronation of Henry of Anjou. Its character was revealed with special clarity when the king's obligation to protect both the Evangelical and the Catholic religions was solemnized, the nobles formally stipulating thrice, and he responding thrice. In Hungary, Bohemia, and so on, the custom is the same, but it would take too long to report the details.

This practice, furthermore, is not confined only to kingdoms where the rule of election has remained intact, since a stipulation of this sort is also a regular procedure even in kingdoms where it is commonly thought that pure succession obtains. When a king of France is inaugurated, the bishops of Laon and Beauvais, as peers of the Church, ask all the people present whether it is their will and pleasure to have the designee as king, and there is, accordingly, a statement in the coronation formula itself that the people have elected him. After the people have indicated their consent, he swears that he will maintain the law and privilege of France and the rights of all men generally, that he will not alienate the domain, and so forth. Interpolations have crept into these articles, and they are now very different from the ancient formula, which is extant in the library of the cathedral chapter at Beauvais, and which, it has been discovered, was used by Philip I. But despite these changes, the main point is eloquently expressed. And the king is not presented the sword, anointed, or crowned by the peers (who are adorned with wreaths themselves); and he does not receive the sceptre or the rod, and is not called "king" until the people have so ordered. Furthermore, the peers do not swear fealty until he has given them his pledge that he will strictly keep the law, *i.e.,* that he will not waste the public patrimony; that he will not, on his own discretion, impose or collect taxes, duties, or subsidies, declare war, or make peace; and, finally, that he will not pass public decrees except in the public council. It is also understood that the Senate, the assembly, and the officers of the kingdom are each to retain its own authority and all other privileges that have customarily been recognized in the French kingdom. Hence, when the king visits any town or province, he is obliged to confirm its privileges and to bind himself by oath to maintain their law and custom. This particularly applies to Toulouse, Dauphiné, Brittany, and Provence, which have special agreements with the king that do not make sense unless they are considered the equivalents of contracts.

The oath taken by the early kings of Burgundy is still extant word for word. "I will maintain law, justice, and protection for all." In England, Sweden, and Denmark the custom is almost the same as in France. In the kingdom of Aragon a king who is about to be inaugurated pledges fealty and homage to the person who represents the justice of Aragon, or the public majesty, and who is seated on a higher throne. After many ceremonies involving the *justicia* and the king, there is a reading of the laws and conditions that the king is obligated to fulfill, and then, finally, the magnates address the king in the vernacular as follows: "We who are worth as much as you, and can do more than you, elect you king on these and these conditions. Between you and us there is one whose command is more than yours." Moreover, it is their custom to repeat this formula every three years in the public assembly, lest the king should think it perfunctory or regard his oath as a mere gesture toward ancient usage. And if the king, inflated with pride of station, should grow insolent and should break the law despite his oath, then, by that same law, he is declared anathema, just as Julian the Apostate was once declared anathema by the Church. Prayers are then no longer offered for him, but against him, and all persons are released from their fealty and obligation to him, by the same rule under which the vassal of a lord who has been excommunicated has no duty to obey and is no longer bound by his oath.

[There are similar practices in Castile, Portugal, Leon, and other parts of the Iberian peninsula, as well as in Belgium, Austria, Carinthia, and so on. The custom of Brabant is held especially interesting, since there is an express warning to the king that he will be deposed if he does not perform the specified conditions. The general rule, then, is that almost all kings take an oath that formalizes a compact between king and people.]

But even if these ceremonies, these vows, these oaths did not take place, is it not clear, from the very nature of the case, that kings are created by the people on condition that they govern well, just as judges are established on condition that they do justice, and military commanders on condition that they lead their armies against foreign foes? And if kings become oppressors, if they commit injustices, if they become the enemy, they are no longer kings and should not be so regarded by the people. But, you may ask, what if a ruler forcibly compels a people to take an oath in his favor? What, I answer, if a robber, pirate, or tyrant—with whom, it is held, no legal bonds exist—should extort a promise at the point of a sword? Or are you unaware that a pledge elicited by force is void, and especially when the promise is against good custom and the laws of nature? And what is more at war with nature than for a people to promise a prince that it will put chains and fetters on itself, will put its throat beneath the knife, and will do violence to itself (for this is what that promise really means)? Thus, between king and people there exists a mutual obligation which, whether civil or only natural, explicit or tacit, cannot be superseded by any other compact, or violated in the name of any other right, or rescinded by any act of force. So great is its force that a king who breaks it willfully may properly be called a "tyrant," while a people that breaks it may be properly called "seditious."

The Nature of Tyranny

Now that we have described a king, let us continue with a more detailed description of a tyrant. A king, we have said, is someone who has obtained the kingdom in due form, either by descent or by election, and who rules and governs in accordance with the law. Since a tyrant is the opposite of a king, it follows either that he has seized authority by force or fraud, or that he is a king who rules a kingdom freely given him in a manner contrary to equity and justice and persists in that misrule in violation of the laws and compacts to which he took a solemn oath. A single person can, of course, be both of these at once. The former is commonly called a "tyrant without title" *(tyrannus absque titulo),* the latter, "a tyrant by conduct" *(tyrannus exercitio).* But it sometimes happens that a kingdom occupied by force is governed justly; a kingdom legally conveyed, unjustly. And since justice is here more important than inheritance, and performance more important than title to possession, it appears that a ruler who performs his office badly is more properly a tyrant than one who did not receive his office in due form. Similarly, a Pope who enters office illegally is called an "intruder," one who governs badly, an "abuser." . . .

[The last point is illustrated by further analogies. The usurper *(tyrannus absque titulo)* who governs well is to be preferred to the tyrant-king. Usurpers are subdivided into foreign conquerors; elective kings who illegally make their crown hereditary; generals who turn their arms against their own country; women who have themselves made queen or regent in countries where women are legally excluded from the throne; and high officials who gradually accumulate powers under indolent kings. In this presentation the ungrateful general and the ambitious woman are treated with special revulsion.

The tyrant-king *(tyrannus exercitio)* is described at length, with all of the traditional commonplaces. The tyrant by conduct is self-willed, is devious, lops off the taller stalks of corn, pretends that there are conspiracies against him, shows no respect for princes of the blood, advances low and vicious men, is suspicious of wise and virtuous men, fears public assemblies of any sort, encourages factions among his subjects to weaken them, uses foreign mercenaries, disarms his own countrymen, surrounds himself with bodyguards, foments foreign wars to distract the people, imposes oppressive taxes to keep his subjects impoverished, wastes the public revenue on his favorites, counterfeits religion and concern for the public welfare, and gives the appearance of virtue by deceit. The description of the tyrant-king then concludes as follows:]

Furthermore, as a well-constituted kingdom contains all the advantages of the other good regimes, tyranny contains all the evils of the bad ones. A kingdom resembles aristocracy in that the best men are invited to the royal council, whereas tyranny resembles oligarchy in inviting the worst and most corrupt. If the council of the first is like a gathering of kings, that of the second is a gang of tyrants. A kingdom also resembles constitutional democracy *(politia)* in that there is an assembly of all the orders to which the best men are sent as deputies to deliberate the affairs of the commonwealth. Tyranny resembles lawless democracy, or mob-rule *(democratia seu ochlocratia),* because, insofar as it cannot prevent assemblies, it bends every effort, uses every device of electioneering and deception, to insure that the worst of men are sent to them. Thus does the tyrant affect the posture of a king, and tyranny, the appearance of a kingdom. The shrewder it is at this, the longer it is able to survive. For, as Aristotle says, we scarcely read of any tyranny that has endured a hundred years.

In sum, a king promotes the public interest, a tyrant seeks his own. But since men are only human, no king can have the public interest in view on every question, and no tyrant can exist for long who seeks his own advantage in all respects whatever. Therefore, if the public interest is generally uppermost we may speak of a king and of a kingdom, and if the ruler's interest generally predominates, we speak of a tyrant and a tyranny. . . .

The Obligation to Resist a Tyrant Without a Title

The next question is whether a tyrant may be lawfully resisted and, if so, by whom and by what means. And we shall begin by considering tyranny without title, as it is commonly called. Suppose, then, that a Ninus invades a people over which he has no legal claim and which has not done him any injury; or that a Ceasar subjugates the Roman Republic, his fatherland; or that a Popelus uses murder and deceit in an attempt to make the kingdom of Poland hereditary rather than elective; or that a Bruenhilde takes over the entire government of France for herself and her Protadius; or that an Ebroinus, encouraged by Theodoric's negligence, seizes the governorships of the kingdom and enslaves the people. What is the law in all these cases?

In the first place, nature instructs us to defend our lives and also our liberty, without which life is hardly life at all. If this is the instinct of nature implanted in dogs against the wolf, in bulls against the lion, in pigeons against the falcon, and in chickens against the hawk, how much stronger must it be in man against another man who has become a wolf to man. To fight back is not only permitted, but enjoined, for it is nature herself that seems to fight here.

Next, there is the law of peoples *(jus gentium),* which distinguishes countries and establishes boundaries that everyone is obligated to defend against any person whatsoever. If an Alexander invades a people over which he has no claim and which has not done him injury, it is as lawful to resist him and his mighty fleet as it is to resist Diomedes the pirate who invests the sea with but a single ship. In this situation it is not Alexander's right, but only his impunity, that is greater than Diomedes'. An Alexander pillaging a country may be opposed no less than the vagabond who steals a cloak; an invader battering the ramparts of a city, no less than the burglar breaking into buildings.

Last and most important is the civil law, which is the legislation that societies establish for their particular needs, so that here is one and there another kind of government, some being ruled by one man, others by a few, and still others by all. Some peoples deny political authority to women, others admit them; with some, kings are chosen from a particular line, among others the choice is free; and so forth. If anyone tries to break this law through force or fraud, resistance is incumbent upon all of us, because the criminal does violence to that association to which we owe everything we have, because he subverts the foundations of the fatherland to which we are bound—by nature, by the laws, and by our oath. Therefore, if we do not resist, we are traitors to our country, deserters of human society, and contemners of the law.

Thus, the law of nature, the law of peoples, and civil law command us to take arms against tyrants without title, nor is there any legal scruple to detain us—no oath or compact whatsoever, entered into either publicly or privately. Therefore, when this kind of tyranny occurs, anyone may act to drive it out, including private individuals. . . .

[The *lex Julia** on *lèse majesté* is not relevant here because a tyrant without title is not a prince in any sense. Resistance in this situation is not sedition but suppression of sedition. Among the ancients, tyrannicides were honored as deliverers, while those who failed to act might be considered traitors or deserters.]

These principles apply as long as the tyranny is still in process of formation, as they say; as long, that is, as the tyrant is still plotting, manoeuvring, and tunneling. But once he gets control, once the people, defeated, have bound themselves to him by oath, once the commonwealth, subdued, puts its power in his hands and the kingdom formally consents to the alteration of its laws, he has obtained the title that he previously lacked, and he holds it now not only *de facto,* but *de jure.* For even though the people has accepted this yoke with reluctance (ἑκόν[τι] ἀεκόν[τι] τινὶ δυμῷ), it is right for the people to obey and quietly to accept the will of God, who transfers kingdoms from one hand to another according to His will. Otherwise, there would not be a single kingdom whose legitimacy could not be questioned. Nevertheless, one condition still remains. The usurper who subsequently obtains a title must not be a tyrant by conduct and must govern according to the law. . . .

[Cases of legitimate (and of illegitimate) resistance against usurpers are cited. As long as the fight is going on, the true location of the country is not in any particular person, or even in the majority of the people, but in those who fight for liberty.]

Lawful Resistance to a Tyrant by Conduct

Even more elaborate discussion is needed for the question of resistance to tyrants who, no matter how they came to power, whether by law initially or by force, are tyrants in the exercise of power.

We should remember, in the first place, that all rulers are human and cannot be completely free of passion as long as body and soul are mixed together, and that we should not look for perfect princes but consider ourselves fortunate, indeed, if

---

*See below, note on p. 191.

we have men of middling virtue as our rulers. Hence, if a prince is immoderate on this or that question, if he is unreasonable at one time or another, or if he is not always zealous in the public interest, attentive in administering the law, or energetic in conducting wars, he is not thereby a tyrant through and through. It is insolence in princes to take their fellow men for beasts, since princes do not rule as men do over cattle or as gods do over men but are born to the common fate of all men. But at the same time it is injustice on the people's part to expect their prince to be a god and to demand divinity from merely human and unsteady nature.

But if a prince persistently subverts the commonwealth, if he brazenly perverts the law, if he shows that pledges, covenants, justice, and religion mean nothing to him, or if, finally, he practices all, or the most notorious, of the tyrannical arts we have enumerated, he is properly a tyrant. And by this name (although in very ancient times it did not have evil connotations) he is branded an enemy of God and man. . . .

[A tyrant differs from the merely weak or foolish prince in that the tyrant persists in misrule and is unwilling to hear good advice. Foolish princes too may legally be deposed, but it is not always prudent for a people to assert all its rights. A ruler should not be considered hopelessly illegitimate until it is clear that he will persist in evil ways in the face of repeated warnings.]

Tyranny is like a raging fever. At the beginning it is easy to cure but difficult to detect; afterwards, it is easy to recognize but very difficult to cure. The leading men, therefore, will oppose its beginnings and overlook nothing, no matter how trivial it seems. But if the prince persists, pays no heed to repeated remonstrations, and seems only to be aiming at a situation in which he can do anything he pleases with impunity, then the fact of tyranny is proven, and anything that may be done against a tyrant may now be done to him. For tyranny is not only a crime; it is the worst of crimes and, as it were, the summation of them all. . . .

We have shown, moreover, that kings receive their royal status from the people; that the whole people is greater than the king and is above him; that the king in his kingdom, the emperor in his empire, are supreme only as ministers and agents, while the people is the true proprietor. It follows, therefore, that a tyrant commits felony against the people who is, as it were, the owner of his fief; that he commits *lèse majesté* against the kingdom or the empire; and that he is no better than any other rebel since he violates the same laws, although as king he merits even graver punishments. And so, says Bartolus, he may be either deposed by his superior or punished under the *lex Julia** for acts against the public majesty. But the superior here is the whole people or those who represent it—the electors, palatines, patricians, the assembly of the estates, and so on. And if things have gone so far that the tyrant cannot be expelled without resort to force, they may call the people to arms, recruit an army, and use force, strategy, and all the engines of war against him who is the declared enemy of the country and the commonwealth. . . .

The obligation between prince and people is ever reciprocal and mutual. He promises to be a just prince; they, to obey him if he is one. The people, therefore, is obligated to the prince conditionally, he to the people absolutely. If the condition is not fulfilled, the people are released, the compact voided, and the obligation nullified. The king is perjured if he rules unjustly; the people, if they fail to obey him when his rule is just. The people, however, is absolved from any charge of perjury if it publicly renounces a ruler who would rule unjustly or if it attempts, by force of arms, to evict a ruler who seeks to retain possession of the kingdom in contravention of the law.

The officers of the kingdom, therefore, when all or a good number have agreed, are permitted to use force against a tyrant. And they are not only permitted but obliged, as part of the duty of their office, and they have no excuse if they should fail to act. Let electors, palatines, peers, and the other notables not assume that they were created and ordained merely to appear at coronations and dress up in splendid uniforms of olden times, as though they were actors in an ancient masque playing the parts of a Roland, Oliver, Renaldo, or any other

---

Lex Julia (de majestate) here refers to the general statement of the law of treason and sedition promulgated by Augustus in 8 B.C.

great hero for a day, or as though they were staging a scene from King Arthur and the Knights of the Round Table as they are called; and that when the crowd has gone and Calliope has said farewell, they have played their parts in full. These ceremonies are not celebrated for amusement; they are not *pro forma;* and they are not the games of children who, like Horace, create imaginary kings. Let the magnates remember, rather, that if the role which they receive brings honor, it carries many burdens also. The commonwealth has no doubt been committed and entrusted to the king as its supreme and principal protector, and yet to them also, as its co-protectors. Just as co-guardians (and even honorary guardians) are established [under civil law] to check on the principal guardian and to demand regular accounts from him in order to make sure that these are kept correctly, so these officers are created to supervise the king (who is accorded the position of proprietor only insofar as he promotes the welfare of his ward) and to make sure that he does nothing to the people's detriment. And just as the co-guardians share responsibility for the misdeeds of the principal guardian should they not intervene and take steps to remove him, if his conduct is suspicious; if he refuses to account for his administration to them; if he does not discharge his duties faithfully, acts deviously, and, in a fashion harmful to his ward, appropriates the goods of the latter for himself and treats his ward as though he were his enemy; or if, finally, he is negligent, lazy, or incompetent, and so on; so likewise, the magnates of a kingdom share the prince's guilt if they fail to suppress tyranny, or to prevent it, or to compensate the prince's negligence with energetic activity of their own. Finally, if a guardian does not do for his ward what any father of a family would do in a similar situation, the ward is not receiving due protection, and the co-guardians are obligated to see that he is taken care of more effectively. Similarly, if the prince acts not like the father of a family but plays the role of foreign enemy instead, the notables, with even greater justification, can and should take steps against him.

Let the great ones of the realm remember that although the king has the leading role in administering the commonwealth, they have the second and the third, and so on, each one in his proper place. Therefore, if he plays his part badly, they are not to follow. And if he would ruin the commonwealth, they may not look the other way. The commonwealth is entrusted to them no less than to the king, and they are therefore obligated not only to perform their own duties, but also to hold the prince to his. Finally, as the king promises to protect the public interest, so do they. Therefore, if the king violates his oath, let them not assume that they are on that account absolved from theirs, any more than bishops are absolved if the Pope becomes a heretic who would subvert the Church. Thus, if they conspire with the tyrant, they are liars; if they connive, they are traitors and deserters; if they do not defend the commonwealth from tyranny, they are themselves to be considered tyrants. But they are true patrons, guardians, and princes, as it were, if they use every means at their disposal to provide protection and defense as they have promised. . . .

[These observations are illustrated by examples of resistance to tyrants drawn from the history of the ancient Hebrews, and of the French, Germans, English, and others.]

And is this not true of the Papacy as well? It is said that the cardinals who have elected the Pope or—if the cardinals should not perform their duty—the patriarchs, who, after the cardinals, are also primates of the Church, may in certain cases convene a Council without the Pope's consent and there pass judgment on him. This would apply if the Pope has scandalized the Church by notorious misconduct and appears to be incorrigible; if reformation, root and branch, is needed; and if he refuses to convene a Council, in violation of his oath, and so on. We read in fact that many Popes have been deposed by authority of the Council. And Baldus says that if their abuses are insistent, the first remedy is speech, then herbs and medicines, and, in the extreme situation, stones. For where appeal to virtue does not help, one must prevail by force of arms. And if it is well established by the judgments of almost all the doctors, and by the decrees as well as actions of the Councils, that a Council may lawfully depose the Pope, who nonetheless boasts that he is king of kings, and cries that he is as far above an emperor as the sun above the moon, and even pretends to the authority of deposing kings and emperors as he sees fit, then who can possibly doubt that the public council of a kingdom may depose not only a tyrant and deprive him of his kingdom but also a king who is dangerously mad? . . .

[If the pilot of a ship is drunk, the subordinate officers must assume command. Where the state is in the hands of a raging tyrant, the magistrates must do the same.]

The king, we have said, is not entrusted with the entire administration of the kingdom any more than the Pope, as they say, is entrusted with the entire episcopacy of the Church, but the people give the administration to each of the notables according to his office. It is true, of course, that to insure harmony in the community and to forestall rivalries among the peers, the supreme position in the commonwealth's administration was given to the king. But although the king swears that he will protect the welfare of the commonwealth, so also do the notables, each one for himself. Therefore, if the king or one of the notables breaks his oath and either wrecks the commonwealth or abandons it in time of danger, may the rest of the notables abandon it as well? Is their obligation to come to its rescue now diminished as though they were somehow released from their oath by another's infidelity? Or is it not precisely when others break their faith that they have an even greater obligation to keep theirs, and especially so, since, like the ephors, they were established primarily for this purpose? For a thing is considered to be just when it fulfills its purpose. And if several men are co-makers of a promise, does the default of one remove obligation from the others? And if several guardians do wrongly by their ward, is a single upright guardian among them bound any less to do his duty as a result of the others' dereliction? The truth, in fact, is that co-makers cannot escape the brand of perjurer if they do not try, as far as they are able, to perform their duty in good faith; and a guardian is himself liable to a judgment of abuse of guardianship if he does not bring suit against any of the other guardians whose conduct he has reason to mistrust. Indeed, the right to bring action to remove a guardian for suspected malfeasance is accorded even to a co-guardian who had no direct responsibilities.

Therefore, those who have promised their strength and energy to the kingdom or the empire as a whole, such as the constable, marshals, peers, and so forth, as well as those who constitute a part of the kingdom, such as dukes, marquisses, counts, barons, and so on, are bound to defend the commonwealth as a whole from oppression, or that part of it which the people entrusted to them next after the king. The former should protect the kingdom as a whole from tyranny in so far as they are able, while the latter, as guardians established for the several regions, should protect that part of the kingdom the custodianship of which they have assumed. The first, I say, are obliged to force the tyrant to submit, the latter, to drive him from their confines. . . . [Examples follow.]

But is anyone, no matter how menial his station, permitted to resist? Is Hendonius Sabinus, or Ennus Suranus, or Spartacus the gladiator, or any private subject whatever, authorized to free the slaves, rouse subjects to arms, and then engage in personal combat with his prince, if tyranny seems to be developing? Not in the slightest. The commonwealth is so little entrusted to private individuals that they, rather, are entrusted to the care of the notables and magistrates and are in effect their wards. If, therefore, they are not permitted to look after themselves, they are surely not expected to look after the commonwealth. Private persons, furthermore, have not been presented with the sword, either by God or by the people. Hence, if they draw the sword they are seditious, no matter how just the cause may be.

The people, finally, create the prince not as individuals but all together. Therefore, before individuals may act against the prince, they must receive either a joint order from the representatives of the community, from the officers of the kingdom and of the regions that make up the kingdom, or at least an order from some one of these. A ward cannot bring an action except through his guardian who acts as its author, even though the ward is the real principal and the guardian is taken as the principal only insofar as he promotes the welfare of the ward. In like manner the people cannot act except through the officers to whom they have transferred their authority and power, and who are either the ordinary magistrates or extraordinary officers created in the public assembly. The people, I say, have given their sword to these persons for that purpose and have submitted to their governance and care. Indeed, these magistrates, just like the Roman praetor who judged cases between slaves and masters, are established precisely for the purpose of serving as judges and defenders in disputes between the subjects and their king so that the subjects should not be judges in their own cause. . . .

[The notables should not shrink from violence if the need is clear, since resort to force may be the means of avoiding even greater violence later on. Private subjects must resist passively until summoned to act by a magistrate, at which point it is their duty to follow him. God has given and may still give private persons special inspiration to initiate resistance. But since miraculous signs are less frequent in the present age, subjects should treat claims of inspiration warily.*]

To conclude this part of our discussion, let us say, in sum, that princes are chosen by God and established by the people. Whereas each individual is the prince's inferior, the people as a whole or the officers of the kingdom, who represent the whole, are his superiors. Part of the procedure of creating a prince is a compact—either tacit or express, either under natural or civil law—between the prince and the people that as long as he rules well he will be obeyed well; that as long as he serves the commonwealth everyone will be his servant; that as long as he is obedient to the law all will be obedient to him; and so forth. The protectors and guardians of this covenant or compact are the officers of the kingdom. A king who violates the compact willfully and persistently is truly a tyrant by conduct. In this case the officers of the kingdom are obliged to pass judgment on him according to the law and, should he resist, to expel him from office forcibly where other means do not avail.

These officers are of two kinds. The first, those charged with protecting the kingdom as a whole, such as the constable, marshals, peers, palatines, and so on, should attempt to constrain

---

*The discussion of special divine inspiration has been summarized here because the treatment of this point in the second question is almost identical. See above, p. 156.

a tyrant, and each on his individual initiative if the others connive or collaborate in tyranny. The second, those who govern a district or a region, such as dukes, marquisses, counts, consuls, and mayors, may, on their own initiative, prevent the tyrant and tyranny from entering their district or town. Private subjects, however, may not draw the sword against a tyrant by conduct since he was created not by all severally but by all together. On the other hand, those who intrude without title may be resisted by all without distinction because here there was no compact. And, in general, the same may be done against those who take advantage of a prince's inertness or negligence to rule his subjects tyrannically. So much then for this section. Anything that may be lacking may be supplied from the second question.

The Fourth Question

Are neighboring princes permitted or obliged to aid the subjects of another prince who are persecuted for the exercise of true religion or are oppressed by manifest tyranny?

. . . It is well established, to begin with, that the Church is one, that its head is Christ, and that its members are so close and so harmonious that none can suffer the slightest blow or hurt without the others feeling it and sharing in his grief, as it is taught throughout the Scriptures. . . .

[Harm to any one part of a body may often be fatal to the whole.]

Since the Church is one, it is entrusted to each Christian prince whole and entire. Inasmuch as it would have been dangerous to entrust the Church to any one individual and a violation of its unity to entrust different parts to different individuals, God entrusted all of it to each, as well as each part of it to all. And princes are not only to protect the Church but, as far as they are able, to provide for its extension. Therefore, if a prince should protect that part of the Church, say the German or the English, which is within his territory, but does not help another persecuted part; if he abandons and deserts it when he could send help, he must be judged to have abandoned the Church. For since the Bride of Christ is truly one, he should guard and defend it with all his might, so that it may not be violated or corrupted anywhere. As private persons are obliged to advance the regeneration of the Church by prayer, magistrates are obligated to fight with might and main as well, and whatever strength they have. . . .

[Examples of princes who acted to relieve the distress of the Church outside their own territories are taken from the Old Testament, the later Roman Empire, and the Crusades. Authorities are cited to prove that neglect of this duty is a sin. The persecution of the true Church anywhere is the persecution of Christ in one of His members.]

"Because," says Cicero, "the nature of all men is one, nature herself decrees that each man should wish well for another, no matter who he is, simply because he is a man. And were it not so, human society would of necessity dissolve completely." There are, then, two main principles of justice: the first, that none should suffer harm; the second, that the interest of all should be advanced as far as possible. Accordingly, there are two species of injustice. The first is to commit injustice. The second is to fail to defend another from attack and injury if one is able to do so. To attack another from anger or other passion is to lay violent hands upon one's fellow. Not to defend another and to prevent injury where this is possible are the same as to abandon one's parents, one's friends, or one's country. . . .

In brief, if one prince transgresses the boundaries of religion and justice, a neighboring prince may religiously and justly go beyond the boundaries of his territory, not to despoil the other of his lands, but to constrain him to his proper duty. And if the neighbor does not do so, he is himself irreligious and unjust. A neighboring prince, furthermore, should be at least as willing to help an oppressed people, if its king becomes a tyrant, as to come to the aid of a king, if his people should become seditious. Indeed, he should be even more willing in the first case where there are a great many victims, not just one. . . .

Finally, as tyrants have always existed, so there are many examples in all the historians of tyranny avenged and peoples rescued by neighboring princes. And let these examples be followed by princes of today, whose duty it is to act against a tyrant and against a tyrant over the body as well as a tyrant over the soul, over the commonwealth as well as over the Church of Christ, or else they themselves will be branded, and most justly branded, tyrants.

And at last (to conclude this subject briefly), religion commands us to maintain the Law of God and to defend the Church; justice commands us to use force against the tyrant who subverts the rights of a commonwealth; charity commands us to relieve the oppressed and to lend a helping hand. To deny these duties, then, is to will the extinction and removal of religion, justice, and charity from our midst.

Notes

Introduction

1. Fritz Kern, *Gottesgnadentum und Widerstandsrecht im Früheren Mittelalter,* Muenster und Köln, 1954, pp. 130, 269–278. (Translated with curtailed annotation as Part One of Fritz Kern, *Kingship and Law in the Middle Ages,* ed. and trans. by S. B. Chrimes, Oxford, 1918.)

2. *Ibid.,* pp. 146–149.

3. For a general treatment see Michael Wilks, *The Problem of Sovereignty in the Later Middle Ages,* Cambridge, 1963.

4. *Ibid.,* p. 185.

5. Cecil N. Sidney Woolf, *Bartolus of Sassoferrato,* Cambridge, 1913, pp. 36ff.

6. *Speculum principum ac justitiae,* Paris, 1530 (written 1438–1441), p. 4. The *lex pactionata* and other aspects of Belluga's constitutional views are examined in an unpublished seminar paper by Jon Gandarias, S.J., "The Constitutional Thought of Pedro Belluga," 1968.

7. This formula is suggested by Harold Dexter Haxeltine's comment on Fortescue. "Fortescue's doctrine of English kingship was the doctrine of a monarchy *limited,* though not of a monarchy *controlled;* it was not a doctrine of parliamentary sovereignty." Sir John Fortescue, *De laudibus legum angliae,* ed. and trans. by S. B. Chrimes, Cambridge, 1942, General Preface, p. xlvii.

8. For details of French political, administrative, and ecclesiastical organization in this period, the standard work of reference is Roger Doucet, *Les Institutions de la France au XVIᵉ siècle,* 2 vols., Paris, 1948.

9. The best survey of basic French political trends on the eve of the civil wars is Lucien Romier, *Le royaume de Catherine de Médicis,* 2 vols., Paris, 1925.

10. Doucet, *op. cit.,* Vol. II, pp. 566–567.

11. E. Armstrong, *The French Wars of Religion: Their Political Aspect,* London, 1904, is a brief but lucid account of politics of the period. For comparative aspects, see H. G. Koenigsberger, "The Organization of Revolutionary Parties in France and the Netherlands during the Sixteenth Century," *Journal of Modern History,* XXVII, 1955, pp. 335–351. Various modern interpretations of the period are collected in J. H. M. Salmon, *The French Wars of Religion,* Boston, 1967.

12. *Antitribonian,* published posthumously in 1603. See p. 48.

13. pp. 63–4, below.

14. p. 64, below.

15. See, for example, David Baird Smith, "François Hotman," *Scottish Historical Review,* XIII, 1915-1916, p. 347. Smith's view is based on an ungenerous interpretation of certain requests made to Hotman by Henry of Navarre, du Plessis-Mornay, and others, for a treatise on the general legal grounds of Henry's status as heir-apparent. But see P. J. Blok, ed. "Correspondance inédite de Robert Dudley, comte de Leycester et de François et Jean Hotman," *Archives du Musée Teyler,* Second Series, Vol. XII, 1911, pp. 204ff. for the actual letters.

16. *Disputatio de controversia successionis regiae inter patruum et fratris praemortui filium* (Disputation on the controversy of succession between an uncle and the son of his predeceased brother).

17. Hotman's theory and the complex considerations underlying it are presented in Ralph E. Giesey, *The Juristic Basis of Dynastic Right to the French Throne,* 1961 (Transactions of the American Philosophical Society, New Series, Vol. 51, Part 5, 1961), p. 30ff. On Terre Rouge see *ibid.,* pp. 12ff, and also André Lemaire, *Les lois fondamentales de la Monarchie Francaise,* Paris, 1907, p. 54ff. Hotman's final statement of his views on succession is the *De jure successionis regiae* of 1588.

18. pp. 92-3, below.

19. *P. Sixti V. fulmen brutum* translated as *The Brutish Thunderbolt of Pope Sixtus V.*

20. p. 70, below.

21. p. 65, below.

22. On electoral procedures of the fifteenth and sixteenth centuries, see J. Russell Major, *The Estates General of 1560,* Princeton, 1951, Chap. 4.

23. p. 74, below.

24. p. 73, below.

25. p. 86, below.

26, pp. 67, 80, 82, below.

27. p. 71, below.

28. p. 66, below.

29. p. 82, below.

30. Hotman's *De feudis commentatio tripertita* of 1572 shows no inclination to abolish established feudal rights.

31. So, for example, Beza, p. 110.

32. p. 89, below.

33. pp. 88–9, below.

34. p. 91, below.

35. The fact that Hotman, in the *fulmen brutum* of 1585, asks the parlements to reject the bull of Sixtus V is not inconsistent with this attitude. The parlements are simply called upon to act, but without praise or even routine expressions of respect.

In the edition of 1599–1600, the first part of the final chapter containing the more virulent part of the attack on the parlements and the reference to usurpation by the Senate are suppressed (along with two whole chapters on the rights of the estates in religious matters as illustrated by condemnations of Boniface VIII and Benedict XIII.) These alterations are significant. But we have no reason to believe that they were either done or authorized by Hotman. We know from letters to and from his son that towards the end of his life he was engaged in collecting or cataloguing his works as well as revising some of them. See *Francisci et Joannis Hotomanorum patris ei filii, et clarorum virorum ad eos epistolae,* Amsterdam, 1700, pp. 352, 357, 261. But we are not told which works he revised, and it is not likely that the *Francogallia* was one of them. A new edition had just appeared in 1586, and Hotman died in 1590. The changes of 1599–1600 are clumsy omissions, rather than revisions, which is not in Hotman's style. And they are not continued in subsequent editions. Finally, Hotman could hardly have authorized suppression of the two anti-papal chapters we have mentioned since in letters of 1587 and 1588 he speaks of his intention of writing a lengthy exposé of Canon law. (See Rodolphe Dareste, *Essai sur François Hotman,* Paris, 1850, pp. 28–29, and p. 28, n. 3.) There is no occasion, not even the reconciliation of Henry of Navarre and Henry III in 1589, which was likely to have induced an old Calvinist militant like Hotman to soften his position on issues like these. The more plausible explanation, then, is that the changes of 1599–1600 were introduced either by Hotman's son, who collected certain writings of his father, or, more likely, by Jacobus Lectius (Jacques Lect), who prepared the collection for the printer. The irony, however, is that the heavy-handed changes on the "Senate" fall short of their objective. They were obviously intended to make at least some accommodation to the religious and political settlement more or less stabilized by Henry IV. Yet the theme of restoration is so deeply woven into so many sections of the *Francogallia* that the impact of its original message is hardly changed.

36. p. 49, n. 6, below.

37. p. 70, below.

38. p. 70, below.

39. p. 199, n. 8, below.

40. Hans Baron, "Calvinist Republicanism and Its Historical Roots," *Church History,* VIII, 1939, p. 36.

41. *Bekentnis, Unterricht und Vermanung* (Confession, Admonition, and Exhortation) *der Pfarrhern und Prediger der Christlichen Kirchen zu Magdeburgt,* by Nicholas von Amsdorf, 1550, p. K, ii.

42. *Ibid.,* p. L, iii. An exposition of Amsdorf's thought is provided in an unpublished seminar paper by Mrs. Cynthia Shoenberger.

43. *Institutes of the Christian Religion,* (John Allen, trans.), Grand Rapids, 1949. Bk. IV. Ch. XX, p. 804.

44. On the character of Goodman and Knox's attitude toward resistance as opposed to that of the Huguenots, see Michael Walzer, *The Revolution of the Saints,* Cambridge, 1965, Chap. 3 *passim.* and esp. pp. 108–9.

45. p. 40, below.

46. p. 98, n. 4, below.

47. p. 79, below.

48. p. 104, below.

49. pp. 125–6, below.

50. pp. 127–8, below.

51. p. 128, below.

52. p. 105, below.

53. p. 106, below.

54. pp. 154 195, below.

55. p. 109, below.

56. p. 109, below.

57. pp. 129–30, below.

58. p. 122, below.

59. p. 139, below.

60. pp. 162–3, below.

61. p. 176, below.

62. p. 150, below.

63. p. 166, below.

64. p. 171, below.

65. p. 195, below.

66. pp. 195–6, below.

67. p. 194, below.

68, pp. 152–4, below.

69. p. 197, below. But see also the account of the compact on p. 179, below.

70. Calvin, *op. cit.,* XX, p. 804.

71. p. 108, below.

72. p. 156, below.

73. Among the better-known general studies of political thought in this period are:
J. W. Allen. *A History of Political Thought in the Sixteenth Century,* London, 1928 (reprinted 1957).
Vittorio De Caprariis, *Propaganda e pensiero politico in Francia durante le guerre di religione, I, (1559–1572),* Naples, 1959.
William Farr Church, *Constitutional Thought in Sixteenth Century France,* Cambridge, Mass., 1941.
Pierre Mesnard, *L'essor de la philosophie politique au XVIe siècle,* 1951.
Georges Weill, *Les théories sur le pouvoir royal en France pendant les guerres de religion,* Paris, 1892.

74. See J. H. M. Salmon, *The French Religious Wars in European Political Thought,* Oxford, 1959. The influence on Jesuit theorists of the sixteenth century like Mariana is indirect and is filtered through the League. See Guenter Lewy, *Constitutionalism and Statecraft in the Golden Age of Spain: A study of the Political Thought of Juan de Mariana,* Geneva, 1960 (Travaux d'Humanisme et Renaissance, XXXVI).

Editor's Note on *Francogallia*

1. The best brief biography of Hotman and general survey of his writings is Rodolphe Dareste, *Essai sur François Hotman,* Paris, 1850. Donald M. Kelley is now preparing a new intellectual biography.

2. p. 21, n. 15, above.

3. On this humanist method, see J. H. Franklin, *Jean Bodin and the Sixteenth Century Revolution in the Methodology of Law and History,* New York, 1963, pp. 18–35.

4. *Ibid.,* p. 46ff. See also J. G. A. Pocock, *The Ancient Constitution and the Feudal Law,* Cambridge, 1957, p. 11ff.

5. See Pocock, *op. cit.,* p. 77ff.

6. Ralph E. Giesey, "Why and When Hotman wrote the *Francogallia,*" *Bibliothèque d'Humanisme et Renaissance,* XXIX, 1967, pp. 583–611. Giesey here reverses the traditional opinion, founded on the date of publication, that the *Francogallia* was a *livre de circonstance* prompted by the St. Bartholomew's Day Massacre. He is therefore able to work out the specific connections of the *Francogallia* to the *Antitribonian* and the *De feudis.*

7. On the editions of the *Francogallia,* see *ibid.,* p. 586, n. 1. Hotman himself counted four editions (exclusive of French translations), but according to Giesey, one of them, in 1574, was merely a reprint of the first.

8. An English translation of the first edition was done by Robert Molesworth in 1711 and was reprinted in 1721 and 1738 in a slightly expanded form. This translation is no longer in print.

9. p. 84, below.

Editor's Note on the Right of Magistrates

1. The standard biography of Beza is Paul F. Geisendorf, *Théodore de Bèze*. Geneva, 1949.

2. The Morely controversy is the central focus of Robert M. Kingdon, *Geneva and the Consolidation of the French Protestant Movement, 1564-1572*, Geneva, 1967 (Travaux d'Humanisme et Renaissance, XCII).

3. On the political doctrine of the *De haereticis* see Robert M. Kingdon, "Les idées politiques de Bèze d'après son traitté de l'autorité du magistrat en la punition des hérétiques," *Bibliothèque d'Humanisme et Renaissance*, XXII, 1960, pp. 566–569, as well as Kingdon's earlier article "The First Expression of Theodore Beza's Political Ideas," *Archiv für Reformationsgeschichte*, 55, 1955, pp. 88–99. Irmgard Hoss, "Zur Genesis der Widerstandlehre Bezas," *Archiv für Reformtionsgeschichte*, 54, 1963, pp. 198–213, also contains a summary of the main arguments of the Magdeburg *Admonition*.

4. See Geisendorf, *op cit.*, pp. 116–120 for a brief summation of the evidence.

5. Giesey, "When and why Hotman wrote the *Francogallia*," *loc. cit.*, p. 582.

6. E. Droz, "Fausses addresses typographiques," *Bibliothèque d'humanisme et Renaissance*, XXIII pp. (379–84), p. 380ff.

7. The original title in French is *Du droit des magistrats sur leurs suiets, Traitté très-nécessaire en ce temps, pour adverter de leur devoir, tant les magistrats que les suijets publié par ceux de Magdeburg l'an MDL: et maintenant reveu et augmenté de plusieurs raisons et exemples.* The complete Latin title is *De jure magistratuum in subditos; et officio subditorum erga magistratus.*

8. The relevant documents (which also indicate Beza's consultation with Hotman) are available in various places, including Klaus Sturm (ed.), Theodor Beza, *De jure magistratuum*, Neukirchen-Vluyn, 1965, pp. 14–15.

9. A. A. van Schelven, "Beza's *De iure magistratuum in subditos*," *Archiv für Reformationsgeschichte*, 45, 1964, p. 74.

10. Henri-Louis Gonin (trans.), Theodore Beza, *Concerning the Rights of Rulers over their Subjects and the Duty of Subjects Towards Their Rulers*, Capetown, Pretoria, 1956.

Editor's Note to *Vindiciae*

1. The complete title is *Vindiciae contra tyrannos, sive de principis in populum, populique in principem legitima potestate,* Stephano Iunio Bruto auctore. It appears under a false Edinburgh imprint.

2. The two most complete surveys of the evidence (both in favor of Mornay) are Max Lossen, "Über die Vindiciae contra tyrannos des angeblichen Stephanus Junius Brutus," *Sitzungsberichte der bayerische Akademie der Wissenschaften zu Munchen,* 1187, Vol. 1, pp. 215–54, and Albert Elkan, *Die Publizistik der Bartholomäusnacht und Mornays "Vindiciae contra tyrannos,"* Heidelberg, 1905 *(Heidelberger Abhandlungen zur mittleren und neueren Geschichte,* Vol. 9), pp. 60–123. A brief summation of these arguments in English is Harold J. Laski (introduction), *A Defence of Liberty Against Tyrants,* Gloucester (Mass.) 1963, pp. 57–60. (Original edition, 1924.)

3. Yet as late as 1930 there was still some sentiment for the exclusive authorship of Languet. Thus Ernest Barker, "The Authorship of the *Vindiciae contra tyrannos,*" *Cambridge Historical Journal,* III, 1929–30, pp. 164–181.

4. G. T. van Ysselsteyn, "L'auteur de l'ouvrage *Vindiciae contra tyrannos,*" *Revue Historique,* 167, 1931, pp. 46–59.

5. Arguments from internal evidence of this sort are almost always tricky, as may be seen from the fact that Barker (see note 3 above), arguing from internal evidence, finds clear evidence of Languet's authorship in sections of the *Vindiciae* that Ysselsteyn has no hesitation in leaving to Mornay.

6. The preface to the *Vindiciae* would have the reader believe that it was written by someone other than the author. Elkan leaned to Loyseleur de Villiers (*op. cit.,* p. 72). Ysselsteyn holds that Languet and Mornay jointly authored it (*loc. cit.,* p. 59). Pierre Mesnard would assign it to Languet (*L'essor de la philosophie politique au XVIe siècle,* Paris, 1951, p. 337, n. 2). It seems to me that any of the three could have written in it in almost any combination.

7. Henri Chevreul, *Hubert Languet,* Paris, 1852, pp. 165–167.

8. The standard biography of Mornay is Raoul Patry, *Phillipe du Plessis-Mornay,* Paris, 1933.

9. See note 2 above.